A DREAM DEFERRED A JOY ACHIEVED

FOSTER CARE STORIES OF SURVIVAL AND TRIUMPH

EDITED BY

CHARISSE NESBIT

SBI

STREBOR BOOKS

NEW YORK LONDON TORONTO SYDNEY

Strebor Books
P.O. Box 6505
Largo, MD 20792
http://www.streborbooks.com

ISBN-13 978-1-59309-125-5
ISBN-10   1-59309-125-7
LCCN 2007938597

First Strebor Books trade paperback edition November 2007

Cover design: www.mariondesigns.com

10 9 8 7 6 5 4 3 2 1

Manufactured in the United States of America

For information regarding special discounts for bulk purchases,
please contact Simon & Schuster Special Sales at 1-800-456-6798
or business@simonandschuster.com

DEDICATION

Dedicated to kids in the system who think they are forgotten,
to my mother who was brave enough to seek help when she could no
longer help us, and to my foster mother, Grace Mary Wise,
who stepped in and took over when we needed it most.
May she rest in peace.

SPECIAL THANKS

To Zane for seeing the vision I had with this book and giving me the forum to live out this dream I've had for a while. It's a small step in changing the way the world views foster kids, but it is a start. Also to Glenda Clare for all of your help in tracking down the organizations that appear in the resources section of this book; Leslie Robinson and Loretta Chan for making me aware of *Represent* magazine. To all of the people who participated and shared their story in these pages, especially my siblings who are not writers but told their stories more eloquently than I ever could. I literally could not have done this without all of your input. Thank you for your honesty and willingness to help others by sharing your experience.

INTRODUCTION: WHY I'M DOING THIS

My journey to compiling these stories began in the fall of 2000. While passing a newsstand, I was greeted with the face of a sad, indigent child whose large eyes and withdrawn appearance instantly drew my attention and forced me to stop and take notice. Upon closer inspection, I could see fading bruises on his frail body, and a look of hopelessness on his face that no child that young (he appeared to be four or five), should ever have to experience. Though this image grabbed me initially, what I saw next hit me harder still. Under his picture in big bold letters was the statement: "The Shame of Foster Care." I rolled my eyes and shook my head. *Here we go again*, I thought. Not the reaction I'm sure the publishers were going for, but their efforts did have one desired effect: I ended up purchasing the magazine. Not because I believed I would be enlightened by the story, but because I needed to know why. Why is it that the foster care system doesn't seem to exist to the world as a whole until a child dies? Why does everyone wait until after the fact to examine the problems most ignored all along, hoping they'd go away on their own? My biggest why, is why doesn't anyone highlight the kids who do survive? Where are their stories? We all know the problems, but little is offered in the way of solutions. I don't claim to have any, but upon seeing the problem in the face of a little boy on a national magazine because of his extraordinary death, I decided to make it a point to celebrate life. This book is my celebration.

As a former foster child, I've never found much reason to disclose how I was raised to those around me growing up. Questions about my "parents" were often dodged or cleverly disguised to give an appearance of normalcy. How could I explain that I'd never met my father, and that while my mother was alive, she was seldom around? I was fortunate to still have contact with my family while in foster care, but make no mistake, my full-time home was with my foster mother in rural Maryland. Because of my proper speech and assumed "uppity" upbringing, no one every questioned that I'd received anything but a privileged, sheltered existence during childhood.

While my childhood wasn't extremely hard, I can say it wasn't exactly idyllic. I was taken care of, but I still missed being with my real family. In spite of this, the bottom line is: foster care saved me. My worst memories from childhood occurred before foster care, yet when probed about my upbringing, I'd intentionally neglect to mention that my "aunt" and "uncle" were actually my foster mother and father. Because of the stigma on foster care in the media, I was afraid to come clean. Afraid I'd be branded as "unwanted," or "unloved." Afraid of having two strikes against me before I even got up to swing the bat, I've finally come to the conclusion that saying nothing was the worst thing I could have done. This is why I've chosen to speak up and have asked others to do the same.

I've managed to accomplish some things in life that I am very proud of: I've finished college, self-published my own book a few years ago, and I am now working for a very well-respected film company, Lionsgate, in Hollywood. I owe a lot of what I've become to the opportunities provided to me by the system. To continue to deny that the system helped me, would be a travesty on my part, and a disservice to other foster kids currently in the system who may feel shame about their plight as I did. As a child you can't control where you came from, but as you grow, you can control where you go. Because of where I've come from, I also feel as though I have nothing to lose, so I live my life to pursue my dreams. I've already seen what can happen when you deny yourself that opportunity and I've vowed not to deny myself the right to try just about everything

I've ever wanted to do. This book is one of those things. I've always wanted to speak out for the foster kids who have managed to not only survive, but to thrive, and now I have that chance. I believe that where you come from does not need to dictate where you can go. Living that reality has kept me on the path to always reach for and attain more in my life. I could have stopped growing or could have stopped pursuing a higher education or status in my life, but there was no need. I still have a lot more to do. I survived the system, and have even thrived because of it, and I'm not alone.

In this book there are many stories. Some are full of hope, some of fear, triumph, and love. Some are from foster kids, some from adopted kids; others are from biological kids of adopted and foster parents. I wanted to include as many different stories as I could since foster and adoptive care stories touch many different lives. People who you thought you knew you may discover anew: successful writers like Deborah Gregory, creator of the wildly popular *Cheetah Girls* book series; and actors such as Christian Keyes, star of several of Tyler Perry's hit stage plays. There are also kids currently in the system, and adults who found their way out and on to success. Whether we may realize it or not, most of us have been touched in some way by a former foster or adoptive child. It is time to acknowledge our gifts and contributions, as well as our never-ending fight to show that in spite or where we came from, or maybe because of it, we've pulled through, persevered, thrived, and most of all, survived.

TABLE OF CONTENTS

FAMILIAR NAMES

Walter Dean Myers.. 1

Deborah Gregory.. 9

Christian Keyes... 19

Woe is Me.. 25

Jessica Holter... 27

Chris "Kazi" Rolle.. 33

Why Did You Go?... 37

FIVE

Can't Stay in the Box... 45

Temporary Stay.. 51

Everyone Wants to Be Loved.. 55

Finding Home.. 61

All Grown Up.. 69

They... 75

REPRESENT

Finding My Father.. 81

Learning To Love Again.. 89

Great Expectations.. 93

Goodbye, Harlem.. 101

Me vs. The World.. 107

OTHER VOICES

Borrowed Siblings... 119

Riding the E-Train to Here.. 131

My Life: The Child of a Foster Mom............................... 145

Trial Basis.. 153

All Else Aside: Jerry and Me... 161

...And Nothing Else and Nothing More............................. 169

September 1986.. 173

The Pride of Foster Care... 179

RESOURCES.. 195

FAMILIAR
NAMES

Walter Dean Myers

Walter Dean Myers is the author of over eighty books for young adults and children. Honors he has received for his books include several American Library Association Best Books for Young Adults Awards and Citations, as well as several Coretta Scott King Awards for Fiction. Though never formally adopted, he was taken in by the Deans at the age of two, and remained with them until he entered the army at seventeen. In his essay "My Life with the Deans," Myers examines the differences between himself and his foster parents that divided him in his youth, yet ultimately informed who he would become as an adult. While in foster care, Myers admits he often felt doubts about himself that he thought had to do with his situation. He says, "I wish I had known my doubts were universal and had little to do with my foster family. Children with their natural parents also have doubts. My accomplishments as an author are grounded in the security, love, and discipline I enjoyed in foster care."

MY LIFE WITH THE DEANS

By Walter Dean Myers

As a child living with the Deans in Harlem I didn't think much about my biological parents. I knew my mother had died when I was an infant and that my father lived in another state. I had no memory of either and no real reason to wonder what they were like. Mrs. Dean, the woman I called "Mama," was a loving woman. It didn't bother me that she wasn't African American because I wasn't sure what that meant anyway.

Occasionally, I did imagine living with different parents, walking into a room and seeing someone who would be a large image of me. There would be the shock of recognition as I saw my own features in another face. Perhaps the imagined parent would smile the same way that I did when I was pleased, or find the same kind of joke amusing. There were no regrets about being a foster child because I had never really known any other state.

As I grew older I knew the Deans were not like me in many ways. I was considered "bright" by New York City School standards and neither of my parents had completed grammar school. My mother read sparingly and I never saw my father pick up even a newspaper. The differences, I felt, were due to the times when we grew up. My father was a black man growing up in the era of strict segregation. His father was a tall, forbidding man with ideas more suited to the nineteenth than the twentieth century.

The Dean side of the family was a colorful, but rather rough, bunch. Herbert Dean had been raised in Baltimore, Maryland and had been working to support himself since he was nine or ten. My Uncle Lee, Herbert's older brother, was in prison somewhere in Maryland. One of his sisters was a marriage broker and had been in a series of fights that I knew about. There were cousins galore. Most of them were Garment Center workers and firmly entrenched in New York's underclass.

Florence Dean was the daughter of a German immigrant mother and a white Native American father. She had been ostracized as a child for being partly "Indian," and later for marrying a black man. I remember being terrified about being taken to visit the Indian and was greatly relieved not to be scalped or otherwise manhandled.

My identity suffered a great deal during my teen years. By then I had been taught and accepted the American value system and had come to the logical conclusion, which I was meant to understand by the school system, that African Americans—we were actually Negroes at the time— were less valuable than Americans with a European Caucasian back-ground. My Harlem environment supported this thesis. Except for the few musicians that lived in my neighborhood, there was no one whom I would find in books. No George Washingtons lived on Morningside Avenue, no General Eisenhowers or Winston Churchills, either.

By the age of fourteen I had discovered books and had decided that my true identity would be in the inner intellectual life. This pleased my foster parents, although their ideas of what I could do with this intellectual life did not coincide with my own.

"You work hard and study your books and you can get a good job in the post office," Herbert Dean often said.

Mama was proud of everything I did and showed it, but when I began to have trouble finding myself she didn't have a clue about how to communicate with me. With typical teenaged arrogance I dismissed her as being old-fashioned, overly conservative, and completely out of touch with the current trends of the intelligentsia. When I was sixteen and my grandfather came to live with us, placing an enormous burden on an already hopelessly stretched janitor's salary, I realized that I would not be able to go to college. I became increasingly alienated from my parents and dropped out of school at fifteen, then again at sixteen. On my seventeenth birthday, I joined the army.

My subsequent development was as different as I imagined and wanted it to be. After some years in the military at the beginning of the Vietnam War, I knocked around a bit and slowly began a writing career. In time I reconciled with my parents, more than a little ashamed that it had been their poverty, and not their lack of sophistication, that had been the root of the differences between us. That and my own lack of maturity.

My parents never changed my name to Dean. Taking in children who needed a home was common in both the white and black communities when I was a child. There was no need for a great deal of formality. So I remained Walter Milton Myers and my first book, *Where Does the Day Go?* was published under that name. But by then I was understanding that it was not my parents' fault that I had stumbled so through adolescence, and I mentioned to an editor, Miriam Chaikin, that I wished they had changed my name to Dean.

"Why don't you change it on your books?" she asked.

So I became Walter Dean Myers for the next eighty-four books. Still, I was thoroughly convinced that I was radically different than these well-meaning people who took me into their home so many years earlier. I was, after all, an intellectual, a successful author earning many times more than my father ever dreamed of having as an income, and totally self-assured of my place in society. I was even trying to rectify some of the omissions in literature that I had suffered as a child. Then came the day when I was chastising my youngest son, Christopher, and my entire perspective changed. Christopher was twelve, nearly six feet, and, in a peak of anger, decided to answer my complaints with one of his own.

"You sound just like Grandpa!" he hurled at me. "You say every thing that Grandpa says."

I dismissed him at first but when I mentioned his statement to my wife, she grimaced slightly and repeated the charge.

"If I hear you say, 'If you want something done, get up and do it yourself,' one more time..."

My invitation to continue the conversation led to a flood of recited "Grandpa-isms" of which I was being accused. I began to rethink how really different I was than those poorly educated folks who had found their way from Baltimore and rural Pennsylvania to Harlem.

What I discovered was that my foster father's philosophy, the idea of action being the core of life rather than dreaming or hoping for improvements, was well ingrained in me. Herbert Dean had no sympathy for people who looked to others for help when they could have affected positive changes for themselves. Now, when I look at what I have done with my life, I see an intellectual side, but I know that most people are as bright as I am, and many have as strong an academically shaded bent. There are even more who are artistically inclined and vastly more gifted than I am, but few who are as prone to action. In my household in Harlem you were expected to pick up any papers on the floor, to sweep up any dirt, to replace anything that needed replacing. In that Harlem walkup there was no other way considered. You did what you knew needed to be done and it was everyone's job to see the need.

My father's idea of "manliness" was to provide food for the table and to maintain a decent place to live. Whenever he saw anyone, men in particular, failing in this aspect or relying upon government help when they were able-bodied, he would call it to my attention as someone who was failing and would restate his reasons. As my wife and son repeated these reasons as coming from my lips, it brought Herbert Dean's words back to me.

My father died without learning to read and that formed a barrier between us that brought him shame during his life and me shame that I didn't realize it until after he had passed. The man who raised me died intestate, and because I was never officially adopted I didn't get any of his possessions. Not the house, not the furniture, not even a memento of our relationship. But what I did receive from Herbert and Florence Dean was a philosophy that has served me well, that has been a source of strength to me throughout my life. What's more I have had a career in the arts that they would have been proud of even from the distance created by their deprived childhoods. I know that it was their love for me, their teachings of self-respect and self-reliance, that form the base for my successes as an author.

Whenever I autograph my books and sign my name as Walter Dean Myers, it is with enormous pride and gratification. I am proud of my own accomplishments and proud and grateful for all that I have been given.

DEBORAH GREGORY

Deborah Gregory is the author of the highly successful *Cheetah Girls* book series which won a 2001 Blackboard Children's Book of the Year award, and has become a popular movie on the Disney Channel, spawning an equally successful sequel. Ms. Gregory is also a freelance writer who was a frequent contributor to *Essence* magazine. A product of the New York City foster care system, she entered at three years old, living in four foster homes and one children's center until she aged out of the system at eighteen. During her time at *Essence*, Gregory often wrote about the foster care experience. In her essay "Savasia's Story," originally published in *Essence* magazine several years ago, the story of a child aging out of the system and the challenges she faces are timeless and still relevant today as no real solution has materialized to make it easier for children transitioning into living on their own. Ms. Gregory feels there is at least one possibility that could make this transition smoother. She says: "Every kid in foster care needs a mentor, a constant person in their life who provides emotional support. There is nothing anyone can say unless they are part of the kid's life. That's what foster kids need and often don't have."

SAVASIA'S STORY

By Deborah Gregory

On the surface, Savasia Simmons seems like your average teenager—lively, friendly and full of effervescent chatter when she talks about her boyfriend, Michael ("The first time I saw him I got whiplash, I turned my head so fast to look at him!") But look closely and you notice something different about Savasia, a spiritual depth that belies her eighteen years and an inner resilience that is an odd mix of courage and emotional vulnerability. One often sees these traits in soul survivors, those whom life has called to walk through fire and drink from a well deep within in order to keep on walking. In Savasia's case, that has meant surviving the destruction of her family, living through a childhood spent in nineteen foster homes—and making sense of the aftermath.

Thousands of teenagers, like Savasia, are living with the complicated legacy of foster care. New York City's foster-care system alone has more than 18,000 children (as of 2005), the vast majority of them Black and Latino. There are more Black foster children now than when I aged out of the same system more than thirty years ago—the result, officials say, of the rise of a drug called crack and the deterioration of the Black family structure. Savasia's young life is a case in point. I found Savasia through a family-services agency in New York City. My request was simple: Put me in touch with an African-American girl who has recently aged out of the system.

On the day that I am to meet Savasia, I wait for her at the Patchogue, Long Island train station. I realize I have no idea what to expect. Will she be disheveled? Will she seem broken or hostile? The faces of foster kids I lived with in four foster homes race through my mind. I think of Jimmy, that surly teenager who didn't speak to me for the entire eighteen months we lived under the same roof. And I still burn at the memory of that conniving klepto, Princess, and the unmitigated gall with which she pillaged my toiletries.

Imagine my surprise when a poised young woman, with sunglasses perched on her braided hair and a Chanel-style, pearl-handled bag clutched in her hand, approaches me and asks, "Are you Debbie?" She's so well spoken, so graceful and pretty, I think, then realize that this is the same reaction caseworkers had on meeting me when I was a teenager. Unwittingly I, too, have harbored the stereotypical image of the poor, damaged foster child who just shuffles along in life. I share my thoughts with Savasia, and we laugh and hug each other, then walk to a nearby restaurant. I notice how well put together Savasia is: her smooth, ebony complexion is powdered to perfection, burgundy lipstick accents her brilliant white teeth and she's sporting hazel contact lenses. Wearing a striped minidress that flatters her petite figure, silver bangles on her wrists and white sneakers without socks on her small feet, she is a picture of urban chic. Over pizza and Coke, Savasia tells me that her fashion sense comes from her mom, Queen Esther Simmons, who was originally from Savannah.

"My mom loved to dress nice," she says. "No one can say Queen Esther was a bum, even though things got really bad toward the end." Savasia was one of three children born to an alcoholic and drug-addicted mother. She has an older brother, Derrick, and a sister, Stephanie. Stephanie and Savasia lived with their mother in a drug-infested apartment building in the South Bronx; Derrick lived with their grandmother in East Harlem. "My mother was heavily into drugs; she tried everything," Savasia shares. "And when crack came out, she went a little crazy." She delivers these details matter-of-factly. Between bites of pizza, she adds, "My mother used to blow smoke in my face and say, 'Here, baby, you want some?'"

Queen Esther had a steady stream of tricks traipsing throughout the apartment to support her habit. Ronald Bailey, Savasia's father (but not Stephanie's), who was originally from Nigeria, spent most of his time in jail. "I used to love visiting my dad in Riker's Island," Savasia says, pulling out a picture of her mom, dad and herself at age six—the last time the three of them were together. I observe how carefully Savasia puts the photograph, a crinkled Polaroid, back into her wallet. I do not mention that I, too, carry in my wallet the only picture I have of my mother. That photograph has developed magical powers for me: Although I haven't seen my mother since I was three, I find that staring at her image evokes ancestral spirits at moments when I feel so lost I don't remember where I'm from. Savasia hasn't seen her mother since she was eight, but it's obvious that her mother's image, too, has taken on a mystical, almost saintly quality.

Not an ounce of anger or resentment surfaces in Savasia's voice as she talks about her tragic life with her mom. She tells me how, when she was six, it was her job to clean the apartment, cook meals and take care of her mother. Prone to physical violence, Queen Esther once hit Savasia in the face with a belt buckle, permanently scarring her right eye. After this incident, Savasia's baby-sitter, a neighbor, contacted child-welfare officials. Savasia's eyes glint with anger. "As soon as I found out those people were coming to our house, I cleaned, cooked and made everything look normal," she says.

The child-welfare workers were fooled. They came in, asked Queen Esther a few questions, then cornered Savasia. "They asked me if my mother hit me," Savasia remembers. "I told them no. They asked me if my mother used drugs. I said no. I denied everything. I didn't want them to take me from her." The caseworkers left, and it wasn't until Savasia was eight that they returned. By that time there was no covering up that something was very wrong in the Simmons's household. Queen Esther had withered to seventy-five pounds, and she was smoking five or six vials of crack a day. Strange men were in and out of the apartment all the time, and one of Queen Esther's drug tricks had raped Savasia. The same concerned neighbor again called child welfare, but the act earned her no thanks from

Savasia, who says bitterly, "I blame that nosy woman for ruining my life."

Savasia describes the day that two caseworkers showed up at her school with Queen Esther in tow: "Right in front of my mother, this psychologist asked me, 'Savasia, do you want to stay with your mother and get beaten, or do you want to leave?' My mother was standing so close to me I could feel her trembling. The whole scene was devastating," says Savasia, who doesn't recall what she told the officials. She does recall that she and her mother were dragged away screaming and crying—in different directions. The last time Savasia saw her mother was in child-welfare court several months later. Feelings of pure powerlessness and foreboding about her future filled her.

"The last place on earth I wanted to go was to a foster home, but I didn't feel I had a choice," Savasia says. There weren't any known family members who could take her. Her grandmother had died of a heart attack, her uncle of a drug overdose and her aunt from a brain injury. Somehow, Savasia says, it's easier to accept that she was placed in the system because she had no extended family. I know what she means. One of the pains I still harbor is the knowledge that my mother's large family in Henderson, North Carolina, was contacted when she was institutionalized—yet none of them would take my two sisters and me.

Savasia and her sister were separated. Until an appropriate group home could be found for her, teenage Stephanie was sent to stay with their brother, Derrick, who had returned from a stint in the army and was living in Montana. Savasia, after a brief spell in a holding station, was placed in her first foster home, in the care of a Jehovah's Witness named Mrs. Vance (the names of foster parents have been changed.) "Mrs. Vance was a beautiful, dignified-looking woman," she recalls. "When we would walk down the street, people used to stop her and ask, 'Are you Diana Ross?' She was a very religious woman, and she took me to church regularly."

Shifting her gaze, Savasia adds hesitantly, "There was another foster child in the home named Natalie. It was clear Mrs. Vance favored her because she was light-skinned and had long hair. I felt dark and ugly because I knew I was only there to be Natalie's playmate." Savasia claims

Mrs. Vance was also physically abusive. "The only difference between my mom and Mrs. Vance was that she beat me under the pretense of religion," she says. "What I don't understand is, if you take a child out of an environment you consider unfit, why put her with someone else who does the same thing?"

After three years with Mrs. Vance, Savasia got tired of the beatings and ran away. Upon her return after a two-week disappearance, she was removed from the care of Mrs. Vance, whose license was subsequently revoked. (Savasia says she recently discovered that this woman has divorced, remarried and obtained foster children in another state.)

Savasia next went to live with Mrs. Herndon, an elderly widow. "She was such a nice older lady," Savasia says. "But I stayed there only for seven months until they found a permanent foster home." Almost thirteen, Savasia was then sent to her third placement, with Mr. and Mrs. Daniels, who were also Jehovah's Witnesses. By this time, Savasia had entered a rebellious period and could be provoked to fits of anger. Her hopes of returning to her mother vanished when her social worker told her that Queen Esther had died in a city shelter six months after Savasia was placed in foster care. Foster care had become a permanent situation, and Savasia wasn't happy about that.

One day Mrs. Daniels reprimanded her for disobedience, and Savasia snapped, "You can't hit me! You're not my mother!" Mrs. Daniels retorted, "That's right, I'm not your mother. Your mother is a crackhead." Says Savasia: "I felt all the rage build up inside me, and I began scheming a revenge." She waited until her foster parents went to bed, then poured gasoline in the living room and lit a match, setting the house afire. No one was seriously hurt, but by the time she made it to the group home where her sister, Stephanie, was staying, the police were waiting to arrest Savasia and place her in a juvenile hall.

Even a hardened Savasia was no match for the rigors of juvenile hall. "That place scared me to death," she admits. "They put me in a dark room and hit me while saying, 'You think you're a bad ass; we'll show you.'" Savasia was referred to therapy and readily agreed to go. After several more brief foster-care placements, she went to live with the Jeffersons in Queens, where she was required to attend regular therapy sessions. But Savasia soon grew wary of the therapy provided by foster care. "I spilled my heart to the therapist, and she betrayed my trust," she says. "One day I came home and my foster mother said, 'You want to go running your mouth to a therapist? You can go sit by yourself in the corner.' It was as if I wasn't a part of the family anymore. I couldn't handle it."

Savasia did eventually master the art of survival in foster care. "I got more control over my emotions," she explains. "So once I had left a foster home, it became a memory. If I had let all the trauma and abuse affect me, I'd be in an institution by now." Not all of the families have been forgotten, however. There were the Mitchells with whom Savasia lived for five months. "There weren't fathers in most of the foster homes, but Mr. Mitchell became a father figure to me," she says. "He treated me like a person. He would ask me what I thought and praise me for being strong. I loved him to death for that." Savasia still calls him "Daddy" and sends him cards on Father's Day. Unfortunately, she didn't get along with Mrs. Mitchell. "I don't think she understood my relationship with her husband," Savasia muses, then shrugs. "I had a lot of personality conflicts with people in the foster homes."

The other placement Savasia recalls fondly was with Mrs. Loomis, the only White foster parent she lived with. "I called her Mommy, and I know she genuinely loved me, so it was very hard for me to leave her." But her foster mother shared a one-bedroom apartment with her sister and brother-in-law. "One night I woke up and her brother-in-law was on top of me trying to rape me," recalls Savasia. "I'd already been raped once, but now that I was older I wasn't going to let it happen again." Afterward Mrs. Loomis begged her to stay, but she says, "I couldn't live there anymore—I was afraid to go to sleep at night."

Nineteen foster homes later, Savasia can look back and admit a simple truth: "I lost my family, and none of these people could give me back what I really wanted—to be with my mother and sister again." For the past year, she has lived with her boyfriend and his family in Long Island.

She met Michael while in a foster home in Riverhead. It was his idea that they live together, and Savasia says his family has been very supportive of their union.

Since her "emancipation" (aging out of the system), Savasia says she has contacted most of her foster parents and tried to make amends. "I've apologized for any pain I may have caused them," she says seriously. "I found it very scary to live with people I didn't really know, and I think that foster parents are scared, too. They are worried about the emotional or behavioral problems that a foster child may bring into their home."

Savasia says she never became accustomed to being called a "foster child": "I hated those words. They made me sound like I was somebody else's hand-me-down." I ask her if she thinks being adopted would have helped her. Savasia seems repelled by the idea. "Adoption is fine for babies, but not for young children or teenagers," she states. "Why would I want to be adopted? I had a mother. Nobody was ever going to take her place." This, oddly enough, is where my experience differs from Savasia's. As a foster child, I secretly pined for two things: Either my mother would return or I would get adopted, acquiring the foster child's ultimate proof of status. After all, I reasoned, adoptive parents don't get paid to take care of you so they must be doing it for love, right?

At the age of eighteen Savasia decided to tie up loose ends. She sought access to her mother's death certificate and learned that Queen Esther died of a drug overdose two years after her daughters were placed in foster care. This information infuriated Savasia. "The caseworker who told me my mother died six months after I went to foster care lied to me," she says, her eyes flashing. "I don't know if it was out of carelessness or just to make placement easier." With her mother forever lost to her, Savasia wonders about her father: "I would like to find him. He could be in jail or dead—but it's important for me to know."

There are still so many stray threads from her past, but Savasia says, "As the questions come up, I will seek answers in therapy." These days she is intent on finishing high school. After that, she hopes to receive a scholarship to attend college in Atlanta, a few hours away from the Georgia town where Queen Esther was born. The desire to trace her mother's footsteps is apparent in some ways. Savasia's career goal is to become a paralegal, a profession her mother had been trained in. But one thing Savasia says she won't do is drugs. "I don't know what happened to my mother in her childhood," Savasia says, "but nobody helped her, and she deteriorated even further after we were taken away. I will never forget what I saw drugs do to her. Never."

The idea of starting her own family appeals to Savasia, and she announces that she'll name her first daughter Queen Esther, after her mother. "Even though my mother is gone, her spirit is with me," she says quietly. She admits the longing for her mother has been more intense lately: "I'm really missing her now because I will be out of high school next year and facing my future."

On this particular day, the very young Savasia Simmons has finished school for the summer and is due to report to her part-time job at a nearby law firm. Our meeting has proved to be a healing experience—and a sad confirmation of the legacy of pain that is randomly bestowed on too many children, in foster care or otherwise. Sometimes I still feel incredibly hurt by not having a family, and my heart breaks for the thousands of children who have known the same helpless sense of not belonging that Savasia and I have lived through. Not all of us survive—but Savasia and I did. As we embrace before we part ways, Savasia tells me we'll be keeping in touch. "I'm never letting you out of my life," she says firmly.

When I suggest that we attend together a meeting of the National Association of Former Foster Children, Savasia's intense eyes brighten. She hadn't known of the organization but is eager to participate. Her reaction brings into focus an image of myself I'd long forgotten: At Savasia's age, I was hardened, bitter and filled with rage. I rejected everything and everyone associated with foster care, no doubt cutting off a few lifelines in the process.

Savasia, on the other hand, has already learned life's most liberating lesson: If you run from your past, it will catch up with you. Better to make peace with your story; better to walk bravely through darkness and into the light.

CHRISTIAN KEYES

Christian Keyes is a talented singer and actor best known for his lead role in the popular Tyler Perry plays *Madea Goes to Jail* and *What's Done in the Dark*. After being removed from his abusive biological home, he found himself in several different foster and group homes, finally finding one that he settled in until he aged out of the system. Determined to not be limited by his harrowing childhood experiences, Christian went on to attend college and write and record his own music, including a song about his parents, "Woe is Me," which is also featured in this anthology. In the following story, Christian tells of the first time he felt truly cared for while in the system, and how that changed the course of his life forever.

MY FOSTER CARE STORY

By Christian Keyes

I grew up in foster care in regular and group homes from the ages of four to six, and twelve to eighteen. The second time around was, in my opinion, the most crucial and life-altering era of my life. It was during this time when various families and single foster parents helped me deal with the terrors of my first twelve years on earth and the lasting impact it had on me. By the age of twelve, the anger, low self-esteem, and complete lack of a sense of self-worth were all beginning to take their toll on me. I was rebelling, acting out, fighting, setting fires, you name it. It didn't seem as though there was much hope for my future, and I myself had long since given up. But it was a foster parent that made me understand why I was doing these things, not a therapist.

Though I don't remember the name of my foster mother at the time, I do remember what she did for me. I had gotten kicked out of school one day and she sat me down and asked me what I was so angry about all the time. She wouldn't let me get up until I answered her, which made me even angrier. I sat and I stewed until she asked me again. Determined not to say anything I sat there, looking through her with angry eyes. I wasn't going to say a word but I couldn't help myself.

"You try being passed around all your life like some second-hand clothes and see how you feel. I hate myself," I admitted. I didn't mean to say it, but once I started I couldn't seem to stop. I guess deep down I wanted help though I didn't know how to ask for it. Years in different homes had taught me to bottle up my feelings, and now it was all boiling up to the surface.

"I was beaten for years and no one believed me," I said. "I told them but they didn't believe me. It was like it didn't matter that I was being abused, they just kept sending me back." I couldn't stop by now, so I kept going.

"Everyone I have ever loved has left me, been taken away, or mistreated me. Now you tell me, should I be mad?"

I was in tears by now, and in the calmest voice possible, she said: "Is it your fault?"

Before I could think, I yelled: "No, it's not!" It was like I was trying to let the world hear me. I could finally be free to let my emotions out and I wasn't going to miss this chance. Again I said: "It's not my fault! I stood up, crying even harder now.

The first pair of arms that ever mattered grabbed me and confirmed that it was not my fault and that I was going to be okay. To this day I still get emotional thinking about it as my heart is still heavy with all the pain I felt, but from that day on things were a little different and my heart was a little lighter. In the arms of the first foster parent who had ever truly cared, I felt that things could possibly get better for me.

Now don't get me wrong, I didn't change overnight, at all, but at least I now knew why I was so full of rage. It was refreshing to be relieved of the guilt I'd carried around for so long. Eventually I learned to control my rage. I would start catching myself when I was about to let it out. The conversation with her also got me addicted to the relief of talking about my feelings to people I trusted and eventually I could talk about my past without hesitation.

I was moved to another foster home a little while later and I floated in and out of a few more homes, attending five different high schools until I finally settled with Roy and Gayle. I stayed with them from ages sixteen until nineteen when I graduated from high school. Moving around the way I had left me behind in school and I had to make up a semester.

I still had some issues when I went to live with Roy and Gayle, but I also was going to a therapist once a week, to talk about everything. Roy and Gayle held me accountable for my actions and pushed me to try different things. When I fell in love with basketball, they put up a hoop, sent me to camps and supported me. I just recently told them how much they meant to me and how important they were to my success. Oh, did I mention, they were white. It didn't matter to them or me. I was a person to them and that's all that mattered.

Roy and Gayle got me back into church and also helped get me a Big Brother, Cliff Turner (the man who introduced me to basketball). Between the three of them, they kept my backside in line, and I am thankful for it. They were there when I graduated, and it was amazing. They even sent me money for groceries when I was at college. I couldn't have made it without these people. God knew just who to put in my life and when.

The accumulation of love, time, attention, and support is what I got from these wonderful people. Most times, that's all we want as kids: time, attention, and love. I say "we" because inside, I am still that little boy, but I am a much happier version of that little boy. One that is not afraid to love and live and trust. My life is much different now. I smile sometimes so hard my face hurts, but I've made it. Because my life could have gone the other way—that anger and those issues could have led me to prison or worse—I have learned to be thankful for the blessing I now have. God helped me make it; loving, giving people helped me make it; and foster care helped me make it.

WOE IS ME

Lyrics by Christian Keyes

I've been wanting to ask you this since I was 4 years old. Dad, Mom, why did y'all leave me?

I cried when I wrote this, sitting here in this chair, heart full of pain.
I try not to show it, but it hurts when I think about that day...
I can still see the brake lights, from that late night, when you drove away.
You said you were coming back, you never came back. I want you to answer this....

Oh Mother, I don't understand,
How can you say that you love me, with your suitcase in your hand?
And father, answer this if you can,
If you decide to leave, who's gonna show me how to be a man?
Woe Is Me

And you, you call yourself a man, you beat my momma, cheat on my momma.
I used to wish I was bigger so I could take care of you myself.
I haven't forgotten, but I forgive. You don't even know what y'all did.
You all broke the heart of a 4-year-old child and never thought twice about it.

Oh Mother, I don't understand,
How can you say that you love me, with your suitcase in your hand?
And father, answer this if you can,

If you decide to leave, who's gonna show me how to be a man?
Woe Is Me

Nothing on earth could make me, walk away from the best thing God ever
gave me.
My seed, my offspring, my baby…I just don't understand.
But I'm glad it worked out this way, cause it made me the man I am today.
And you showed me the kind of father I should never be.

Oh Mother, I don't understand,
How can you say that you love me, with your suitcase in your hand?
And father, answer this if you can,
If you decide to leave, who's gonna show me how to be a man?
Woe Is Me

JESSICA HOLTER

Jessica Holter is a former journalist, now best known as the creator of the hot poetry company the Punany Poets. A former foster child, she's learned that family is sometimes where you create it, and she calls the other members of the Punany Poets her family. During her years in foster care, Ms. Holter often rejected her new home in favor of trying to regain her mother's affections. In the following poem "Saturday Mournings," she tells the story of how after many missed visits and never fully receiving the love she craved from her biological mother, she finally accepts the love of a stranger, as well as the pain that came with losing her biological mother in the process.

SATURDAY MOURNINGS

By Jessica Holter

Those Saturday mornings
I pushed my bed
Away from the wall
Hoping my sister would not hear
Hoping my foster
Momma
Would not hear
Hoping the old wood would
Not squeak or crackle
Too loud
And tell of my desire
Tell of my weakness
Tell of a
Little girl's dream
To see her
Mother
Tell of a Black Girl's longing
For White arms to be
Intertwined with
Black ones
Tell of brown eyes'
Need to see hazel Irish ones
Tell of the truth

Of how I could
Love you mother
Still need you Mother
Even after
The Give-away
The living away
The way irony played
In your manic rage
On a Berkeley Street
The day you said you needed
To find her
She, Not me
Offering in my palm my whole
Black heart
But SHE, the daughter you never saw
But needed, no less...
The words still echoed in my head
Replay each day
Who?
Wants this little
Girl?
Drunken Toes
Tap, Tap, Tapping
Desperado's cadence
On run over thongs
Who?
Who?
Who wants this Little
Girl?
Wrist burns
Under drunken grip
"The trick" my sister said
"Is to stand the pain"

Twisting my wrist skin
In a game of
Indian chief
"When you can't stand no more, you lose!"
So you gotta howl like
An Indian…Cuuuuzzz You lost!"
Child games
Flashing in my mind
But there is no time
To be a child again
And anymore
But maybe not forever…
And there is no howl
Escaping my lips
Only the train's
Screamiiiing for me
And I want to be on that caboose and go aaaaawayyyy
A lone Panthress
Like the poster picture
Fuzzy beneath my finger
On the basement wall
At foster home
Opens Black bosom to me
"I'll take her…I'll take your Little Girl"
No howl escapes
My lips
The fire of
Your red hair burns my eyes
As you slip into a sea of people and traffic
And your
Battle dress jacket
Slips into loud
Stares of onlookers

The train howls our pain
Saturday mornings
I loved
The loving
To see you
Mother
Cried dry tears
When you did not show
Pushed my bed
Back to the window...
My sister and I played
Indian Chief
Till Pain was
Only
A Game...
I could be a child again.

Chris "Kazi" Rolle

Chris "Kazi" Rolle is a hip-hop artist and community activist born in the Bahamas and currently residing in New York City. Through his work at Art Start, a program which helps at-risk youth channel their energies through the making of positive music, Chris managed to turn his life around, going from a once-homeless teenager, to a revered activist and leader in his community. Recently featured in the documentary *The Hip Hop Project*, Chris continues to inspire others with his story of struggle and perseverance against what seemed to be insurmountable odds. Once abandoned by the mother he barely knew, he has transformed himself into an adult who has learned the meaning of healing through his music and deeds, pushing on in spite of his obstacles, and most of all, the power of forgiveness.

FROM STRUGGLE TO TRIUMPH: MY STORY

By Chris "Kazi" Rolle

I was born in a little island called Nassau in the Bahamas. My mother was a Jamaican immigrant who was trying to get to America via the Bahamas, due to the fact there were less obstacles for Bahamians seeking to come to the United States than there were for people coming from Jamaica.

At six months old, my mother left me in the care of friends to venture to the United States in hopes of opportunity. She had left three kids earlier with my grandmother in Jamaica. She never returned for me. In 1980, the Bahamian Department of Social Services substantiated reports that I was living in an abusive situation. At four years old, I was found wandering in the streets and was subsequently institutionalized at the Children's Emergency Hostel for orphans.

Catherine Brown, a social worker at the hostel, developed a relationship with me and in 1982, I was fostered by her and her family. The adjustment was very difficult—they said that I presented numerous behavioral problems at home and in school, as I could not understand how strangers could love me when my own mother had abandoned me. Thankfully, Mrs. Brown trucked on. I was officially adopted on November 4, 1988.

I still got into a lot of trouble and posed ongoing challenges. Due to lack of the proper resources to help me with my emotional issues, the family came to their wit's end in dealing with me. In 1990, I was placed in the Ranfurly Home for Children. While in the Ranfurly Home, I was placed in a psychiatric ward for unruly children. It was determined by the

Department of Social Services that my challenges were directly related to my early childhood experiences. As a result, the American Embassy was contacted to locate my biological mother and on December 21, 1990, I was reunited with her in New York City, USA.

From 1990 to 1992, my relationship with my biological mother was highly tumultuous. By 1992, at age sixteen, I found myself homeless once again, on the streets of New York City. From 1992 to 1994, wherever I laid my head was my home. Gangs were my family. Warm train stations were my apartment. Street pharmaceutical corporations became my employers. Five-finger discount was how I shopped for clothing. It was all about survival. I found my self incarcerated numerous times. I was on a road to nowhere. All the people who said that I wouldn't amount to anything were being proved right.

In 1994, at age eighteen, I finally decided to get my life together. I enrolled in Public School Repertory Company, a "last chance" performing arts high school, and I discovered that I had a passion for music and theater. It was there that I realized the power of the arts as an outlet for healing. I wrote a play based on my life story called "A Brooklyn Story."

At Public School Repertory, I connected with Art Start, an arts-based youth organization. I also began writing, directing and acting for the award-winning urban theater company, Tomorrow's Future. My play, "A Brooklyn Story," earned me a New York Governor's Citation and a Martin Luther King, Jr. Award. In 1995, I received the CBS Fulfilling the Dream Award for my play and my work in schools and homeless shelters advocating education and drug abuse prevention.

In 1999, having personally experienced the healing power of the arts, I chose to dedicate my life to providing a similar outlet for under-served youth. I created "The Hip Hop Project," an award-winning program that connects New York City teens to music industry professionals to write, produce, and market their own compilation album on youth issues. The program attracted Russell Simmons and Bruce Willis, whose support contributed largely to the success of the program. In 2000, I was featured on the Oprah Winfrey show in a segment called "People Who Are Using

Their Lives." In 2005 I passed the torch of leadership of the Hip Hop Project on to one of my students, and joined the organization's Board of Trustees.

Looking back I realized that there was not just one moment that changed my life. It was a process. Every time I wrote my story or shared it, I slowly chipped away at the boulder on my shoulder. That process was cathartic. I love hip-hop. It healed me and I think it can heal the world so I shared my story on the big screen to hopefully inspire lives. I also share my life in music to touch the hearts of the people that hear it. The following is a song about my story. Imagine a beat while you read "Why Did You Go?"

WHY DID YOU GO?

By Chris "Kazi" Rolle

Abandoned six months & change
my biological she never explained
It wasn't by choice I came
Upon this earth it hurts but I maintained
In a third world country homeless hungry
It haunts me to wonder why my momma don't want me
I don't know sposed to come for the bro no sho
So I keep a lo-pro quite introverted
The verdict wasn't worded
So I settled and reverted to dreamin and pretending
I would meet her and be tensing start screaming and venting:

YOU THE REASON I WAS SENTENCED
FIENDING FOR ATTENTION, NEEDED INTERVENTION
GOT BRUISED BY THE BELT, SKIN TATTERED WITH WELTS
AND NOBODY COULD HEAR ME YELL....

Why Did You Go And leave me all alone
I don't know / But I know I must move on...
with this life...Can't be worried bout you no more
cause it's my fight, my life, my life...

Sometimes I let out a sigh feeling tight inside
wishing I could die she left me high and dry
I don't know what I did to live in an orphanage
unwanted kids we was doing a bid,
nurses they come there, we used to run in fear
hands in the underwear ain't supposed to find them there
days and nights we gaze at the stars
we prayed up to God could escape through the bars
at odds with the most high, inquiries multi, memories they float by
little boys we don't cry, rivers in the ocean got flooded with emotion
said fuck it and revolted cause yo I couldn't hold it
at five got fostered, first time adopted it was really awkward
but we all kinda forced it; they kept it cordial
tried to make it normal but I always felt awful
cause I thought about you often...

Why Did You Go And leave me all alone
I don't know / But I know I must move on...
with this life...Can't be worried bout you no more
cause it's my fight, my life, my life...

Kids at the school was cruel they broke the golden rule
treat me like a fuckin fool, for a kid that wasn't cool
searchin for a buddy lotta people made me worry
gave me looks that was ugly sayin nobody loved me
start to believe it was true, maybe they never knew
didn't have a single clue what their words could do
now that i'm older got a chip on my shoulder

the size of a boulder plus a matching ulcer
I'm carrying weight plus hate on my face
what does it take for you to state you made a mistake
I had to realize the size of your pride meant you couldn't apologize
left your child deprived, feelings I minimize
can't even look me in my eyes cause you know the guilt will rise,
so I just suck it up, move forward and trust my gut
and when emancipated Imma be like whut!...

Why Did You Go And leave me all alone
I don't know / But I know I must move on...
with this life...Can't be worried bout you no more
cause it's my fight, my life, my life...

FIVE

Five

Five is the story of myself and my four siblings. I am very proud to have all five of us together in the pages of this anthology. We all entered foster care together, yet we each have our own unique, separate stories to tell of the experience. My siblings and I don't always speak of our experience in foster care with each other, so the honesty with which they've shared their experiences because I asked warms my heart. Sharing our experience here is about celebrating what we've done in spite of our challenges, and is not about pointing fingers at our extended family for what they may or may not have done. None of the stories in this anthology represents that thinking. Some of my siblings' stories are told through me, others straight from the horse's mouth, but each individual person's story is told through each person's eyes, and from their hearts.

—C.N.

CAN'T STAY IN THE BOX

By Michael Wright
(As told to Charisse Nesbit)

I entered foster care in October of my eighth-grade year, two months before my fourteenth birthday in December. Even though I was technically still a kid, I'd already had more responsibilities than any kid ever should. For quite a while I'd been responsible for my four siblings while my mother worked long hours to try and provide for us, and at times it was too much for me to take. I had to do whatever I had to do to make sure we had what we needed. From working on a trash truck, to stealing food or water from neighbors, to getting oil for the lamps that lit our home when the lights were cut off. I would call my mother collect from pay phones to give her updates, and would try not to think about how much was heaped on me before I had officially reached puberty. As if it wasn't enough that I had to do this on my own, I didn't get much encouragement from those around me. Dealing with our neighbors didn't make life any easier for me.

One family I remember the most, lived at the end of our row of houses. The father owned his own business, and his children felt they were better than us because they had a more privileged lifestyle with both parents at home. I remember them throwing dog food at our house, taunting me because they knew we were poor and often had nothing to eat. I hated them for making fun of something I couldn't help. I did the best that I could, but to them it didn't matter. My siblings and I were dirty, poor, and our parents weren't around. We didn't matter, and therefore, were fair game to be made fun of. For them, being poor made me less worthy of respect, and this was the first time I'd been labeled this way, put in a box that I would spend the rest of my life trying to get out of.

Another box soon came in the form of foster care. Though I wasn't happy at first to be in a foster home and away from the freedom of coming and going as I pleased, I do have to admit that it was nice to not have to carry the load for once. In Aunt Grace's house, there was a mother figure, a father figure, plenty of food, and lights for days. I could finally relax for a moment which was nice, but to me, it still wasn't home. I never felt a part of the family, and I was convinced that my foster mother only wanted me for the money she'd get and the cheap labor. I often felt like a second-class citizen to her biological grandkids. We'd often go to a neighboring town where she would attend an auction, buying up several items I'd have to load into her station wagon and then work until late at night in her house next door to the one we lived in, unpacking boxes and cataloging things for her to sell.

Her grandson helped, but she'd always let him go early and pay him more than she did me. Aunt Grace was a strict disciplinarian, and definitely wore the pants in the family. We had our blow-ups, but in the end, she always got her way. Not used to being dictated to, her strict discipline never sat well with me. I did appreciate our father figure Pop, though I do wish he would have engaged me more and spent more time with us. He was a role model to a point in that he was there and he worked hard to provide, but that was the extent of my interaction with him. We never did the things that fathers do with sons, like go fishing together or play sports. Pop was in his late fifties and was beyond anything more strenuous than working in his garden or cutting the grass. I really needed a father figure in my life, and with Pop's hands-off approach to raising us, I knew I would never find it in him.

Aunt Grace and Pop, while they provided a home and food, they didn't really pay attention to our education. Having grown up in a time when survival was more important than school, neither had actually finished high school, therefore helping me with school work wasn't high on their list of priorities. They did teach me the value of hard work, and work I did. From hauling furniture from the auction, to washing the hundreds of plates she'd bring back from her senior citizens' meetings, I worked. I often felt as though the extended members of our new family looked down on us and didn't appreciate our being in Aunt Grace's life. I remember never feeling like I belonged, until finally, I didn't.

Unable to stand the strict discipline and alienation I felt from the extended family, I made my case to get out. While we lived in a different town when we'd been taken to the foster home, we were still close enough to keep in touch with members of our biological family. I convinced my grandmother to take me in and allow me to stay with her. I never understood why our family never reached out to us before we went away, or even after for that matter. Had I not initiated living with her, it may have never happened. Though I've never called them to task for this, deep down a part of me has never fully forgiven them for not stepping up and volunteering to take us in. It took a stranger to do what they'd failed to do. I've never asked why they didn't fight for us. Not knowing was better for me. At that point I didn't really think about it much anyway. Asking questions would have delayed my progress toward getting what I wanted, and I just wanted out of foster care. By keeping my other questions to myself, the only one I asked my grandmother, was if I could come stay with her, and she said yes. I was happy with that, and finally living with family; out of the "box" that being a foster child had put me in.

Though life after the foster home didn't provide much stability, it was good to be with my real family. Though very nice people, the environment I was in wasn't the best. I saw things I shouldn't have seen, and the emphasis on school work still wasn't present. In spite of this, I pushed on. Over the years, I learned that no matter where you come from or what is lacking, what you become in life is ultimately up to you. The success my siblings and I have achieved has a lot to do with us as people. No one really gave us anything. We had to do a lot on our own. No matter who I was living with, whether it be my foster mother or my grandmother, I was going to do whatever I had to do to get where I needed to be in life. Even if I had to do it myself.

After high school, I entered the Navy, and found myself married with children at a young age. Quite a few things in my life mirrored that of my mother, except I learned from her mistakes and vowed not to repeat them. I don't claim to be perfect in my choices or the ways that I've managed to get by in life, but I've done what I had to do to better myself and survive, and eventually I found myself in the very profession that helped me as a child. After I left the service, I was in a place where I was divorced with two young children to raise. I'd gone to court several times to fight for custody of my kids, and I knew it was up to me to provide for them. I needed a job. I ended up working for the State of Delaware, overseeing group homes for foster kids and mentally disabled adults. I'd visit the homes and see kids like I used to be, troubled and lost, and I'd do my best to make sure they were being treated right.

When I first got into this business, I'll admit I got caught up in how lucrative it could be. I felt like I understood why Aunt Grace took in all five of us kids at once. There could be a good amount of money in it. I often took in disabled adults, having them live in my home for extra money. At first it was a career move, but just as I'm sure happened with Aunt Grace and my siblings who stayed longer than me, the people I took in became family to me, and I learned I was getting more out of the experience than money. I was making a difference. I cared for people who may not have made it on their own in the group homes. In my home, they had a chance to be a part of a family, and my children learned what it was like to experience another side of life. They learned what it is to appreciate the gift of language, and the ability to care for yourself, things the people I often cared for didn't have. They also learned tolerance for the mentally challenged, and often helped me care for the people I would bring home. They understand what it is to not have much, but never to the extent of what I'd experienced. I've managed to give them that lesson without making them suffer as hard as I did for it. I do believe in tough love, and I have taught that to my children. As they grow into adulthood, I want them to learn how to fend for themselves as I did, and understand how to take care of themselves and not expect anyone to give them anything they haven't earned.

For most of my life, I felt that foster care had not benefited me at all. Now when I look at where I am—happily married, a father of three, a bachelor's degree and a successful career—I realize I did learn a lot from my short time in foster care. It was one of the few times where I could truly be a kid and not have to worry about having adult responsibilities. I did feel that other people around me looked down on me because of my circumstance, but that only made me work harder to get past it and become more than they ever thought I'd be. I freed myself from the "box" they'd put me in. I recently saw the same neighbor who had once thrown dog food at me, and her life has turned out to be anything but ideal.

No longer the fresh-faced young girl I remember, she is in her mid-thirties, overweight, and missing teeth. She actually asked me for money, figuring I could help her because according to her: "You live in such a nice house." Ironically enough, this "nice house" is within walking distance of where she grew up, a few houses down from where my siblings and I sat in darkness, wondering where our next meal would come from and how we would get by, while she and her brother taunted us and threw dog food at me for dinner. This was the same girl who had both parents growing up. She had all of the opportunities in the world to be successful. More than I ever did. The same girl who, according to statistics, should be better off than me, but she isn't. I could see this as poetic justice and gloat the way I'd once dreamed about doing when I was a child.

Instead I choose to count my blessings that the hard work I'd endured during and even before foster care taught me to always provide for myself no matter what, and above all, to become someone that my children can say has always provided for them. And even though I haven't been perfect in my methods, they can say without hesitation, that I was there, and because of my efforts, they won't ever let anyone put them in a "box" by limiting their possibilities or endeavors in life.

TEMPORARY STAY

By Tanyita Nesbit Ruley

It was only going to be for six months "they" said, a temporary arrangement until my mother could get back on her feet. When she broke the news that cold morning in October, I pleaded with her to let my older brother and me stay at home, even though no one would classify where we were living as a "home."

"We can use the blankets to keep warm," I'd begged, because I knew at least one of the reasons we were being "forced out" was because we had no heat in our home. Thinking the foster home would have bars on the windows, as one of my cousins had once told me was the case, I feared going. I thought staying in our current situation, though dire, was better than being in a place resembling a prison. I cannot remember the words my mom used to explain the situation to us, I only remember my younger brother crying and clinging to her hip as they stood in the window following her news.

Because my mother worked double shifts as a nurse at the time, we were often left in the care of family members and friends who needed a place to stay. This went on for a little while until the lodgers eventually stopped staying over, leaving us to fend for ourselves. Little by little, our life as we knew it, changed. First, the lights went out, then the water, the heat, and the food, until all basic necessities were eventually non-existent. It happened so gradually that I don't quite remember thinking it was wrong at the time, although the shame of wearing dirty clothes and two nappy ponytails to school was always my cross to bear during those days.

In my new home, I experienced none of the general issues frequently associated with foster care such as abuse and neglect. It was a wonderful experience at the beginning because I finally had three square meals, treats after dinner, a clean bed, fresh braids, and adult supervision. Gone were the bed bugs, hunger pains, roaches, and dirty clothes that were my existence for years. It was at the foster home where I first experienced an African-American church, soul food, Little League sports, Michael Jackson, Girl Scouts, and many niceties that come with being raised in a small close-knit community. My foster parents were in their late fifties with adult children, but they stepped into their role without incident, as they had been accepting children into their home for years.

Though things started out great, as I grew, my relationship with my foster mother became somewhat strained. Though there were no loud arguments or disrespect on my part, for it was not tolerated, I never talked with her about personal issues such as having my first period, school work, or boyfriends, because she was *not* my mother. Though I'd lived with her for years, I didn't feel that closeness with her that should have come with time. Because she was headstrong and proud, she wasn't going to do anything extra to be accepted by me, either. Thus began the holdout and we simply existed in the same house with very little dialogue. She told me when to clean, when to come in the house in the evenings, when to go to church, etc., and I complied. I never showed her any love or affection, and I didn't receive any in return. My foster father was a provider and that was it. If he ever had anything to say to us, it was preceded by a growl.

Although I would have never admitted that anything good came out of my foster care experience while I was there, the minute I walked out the door after high school graduation, fear engulfed me like a dark cloud and I suddenly realized how cared for I had been. All the rules and order were gone and I was truly on my own. As I matured throughout my life following foster care, I realized my foster mother didn't have to take five children into her home during her retirement years. I now find myself saying things my foster mother would say, doing the things she would do, and fortunately for me, all of the examples I received from her were positive. The emotional experience could have been better, however, I realized that if it weren't for my "detour" to the foster home during those critical formative years, the course of my life would have differed dramatically.

Had I spent my teenaged years in the conditions we endured with my mother, I most certainly would have been a statistic. I imagine that I might have been a young single parent, with a high school diploma at the most, no job skills and no future. Because of the structure, consistency, and values that I received from my foster parents, I graduated from high school, served in the United States Army for fourteen years, and completed college. Of our four siblings, two have obtained advanced degrees, one has a bachelor's degree and serves his community as a social worker, I have my bachelor's degree and work as a United States probation officer, and the youngest is an Army veteran who is employed as an operating room technician. My sister, of whom I am very proud, authored this book.

As a result of the foundation that was created by my foster parents for my siblings and me during those seven critical years of my life, I hope we have changed the course of generations of our descendants. Our children are now reaping the benefits of the comfortable, stable existence we have worked hard to create for them....and *they* don't know any different.

EVERYONE WANTS TO BE LOVED

By Shawn Nesbit

Everyone wants to be loved, cared for, to be part of something special. To feel like you were put on this earth for a reason. Sometimes you get that from your immediate biological family, sometimes you don't. Sometimes you are born in a situation where your circumstances and environment can have irrevocable consequences. My four siblings and I were born into the latter situation and fortunately, we were rescued by a family who agreed to take a family of five into their home.

Before foster care, life was hard for all of my brothers and sisters. My mother had five children by three men, and the only consistent factor among them was they were irresponsible with questionable character. Coupled with the fact my mother was young and still did not know who she was or what she wanted out of life, men, or whatever, we suffered the consequences. This instability in my mother's life had its impact on us. Though it wasn't immediate, eventually it would take its toll.

One of the men my mother lived with beat us all for the smallest of offenses. For a select few, he saved an especially heinous crime: molestation. My mother didn't realize what was happening until it was too late. An outburst by a sibling on the bus one day revealed all and though my mother hesitated to believe it at first, it was soon clear that it was the truth. She finally left him, only to move on to a married man who would visit her occasionally at our new home. He stayed around for a while, playing surrogate father for a bit, until he, too, went away, leaving my mother to once again fend for herself and try to keep a roof over the head of her five children.

In trying to maintain this new place by herself once friends and family ceased to help, my mother, overwhelmed by the circumstances, decided to run, burying herself in her work. Though she would still occasionally show her face, overall she was never there as my older brother and sister struggled to care for us. She was present enough to see we were still alive despite our dire circumstances, but not strong enough to do anything to make them better.

At first she'd leaned on different people to look after us, but that caused more trouble than good. There was the overweight babysitter who insisted on cleaning the furniture with kerosene and then "accidentally" lighting it on fire and leaving it to burn on the front lawn, blaming it on my three-year-old brother. At one point one of our aunts and her three children lived with us, but soon they were gone as well. I remember the tough days and months leading up to my brothers and sisters being removed from our "home" and placed into foster care. It was a daily ordeal to survive our conditions. There were the countless days and nights without electricity, water, or food, where we could not wait until school the next day to drink from the water fountain. I remember odd details like being embarrassed and forced to lie about watching *Mork & Mindy*, knowing full well we didn't have electricity to light so much a light bulb than a television. I remember watching our older brother get arrested at the local convenience store stealing chips and soda so we could eat. All the while, not having a responsible adult in the household. Seeing our mother became an event only to be disappointed immediately when she had to go to work. Many of these memories are too painful to recall, but reinforce in me the need for us to be saved. And finally, we were.

I didn't know what foster care was but would quickly find out. My sister and I were in school and were called to the office. Two strangers—a tall, slim black man and a young, Indian woman with an accent and a very pleasant demeanor—were there to take us away. These were our social workers who told us we were going to a better place. I just remember screaming and crying and saying I didn't want to go, not understanding that where I was going was only for my benefit. We drove the sixteen miles or so to this new town we had never heard of, Cecilton, MD. The social workers walked us to the door and the first thing I saw was jars of candies, cookies and all types of goodies. We met our new caregivers, Aunt Grace and Pop. They were both older and we had no idea what to expect. In the home were two other foster children who were both older and had been with Aunt Grace for sometime, as well as her biological granddaughter. Over the years, Aunt Grace and Pop took in over fifty or so foster children, most of them before we'd arrived. Truly amazing when I reflect on it now, but at the time, I did not appreciate their efforts.

Adjusting was not easy in the Wise household. There was so much that we had to learn. We had no stability, no sense of responsibility or manners, and no adults who ever gave us instruction. My hard lesson learned was immediate. I frequently had violent temper tantrums and Aunt Grace, the disciplinarian, would go to all measures to break me of this habit. The "heat for the seat" was a wooden stick we all soon became familiar with, and every single discretion was immediately met with that weapon. The pivotal moment for me though was in the second grade when I had a temper tantrum with a teacher. The teacher said I stabbed her with a pencil of which I honestly pleaded innocent to. Yeah, I had a temper tantrum, but even at the age of seven, I would not compromise my principles and admit to something I did not do. Needless to say, it was my word against hers and Aunt Grace used this as an opportunity to teach me a lesson.

Aunt Grace authorized the principal of the school to not only paddle me, but to paddle me in front of my classmates. Truly, until a few years ago, this was a painful and embarrassing experience. There was also a time when my sister and I were playing around at the praying altar at church. Aunt Grace made us kneel at the sofa for hours on end until we understood the correct behavior. We ended up falling asleep on our knees from kneeling for so long. These punishments were hard to deal with at the time, but they have stayed with me in so many ways. These are lessons I have kept with me today in how I raise my children. There are always consequences for your actions. They can be positive or negative, but understand there are always consequences and you need to be responsible to ensure you determine what kind you will face.

Life continued in the Wise household and every day, month, year introduced my family to new things. Aunt Grace and Pop grew up during the Depression era. In addition, Aunt Grace lost twin children during this period because she didn't have food for them to survive. This was never lost on her or how she would raise the fifty or so children to come through her door in the years to follow. Everything was saved...*every-thing*. Plastic plates, utensils, aluminum foil, and cups from a previous senior citizens event were salvaged and brought home to be washed and then used. Man, was this awful. Aunt Grace also sold used goods from the neighboring house she owned. Regarding school clothes and the like, we got what we needed and nothing more. No-frill foods, government cheese, hand-me-down clothes—was what we received. Only now do I appreciate the lessons we learned. Aunt Grace had to survive. She lost two children and that would never happen to her or others in her care again. This valuable lesson taught me to appreciate what I have, and earned, and to never take it for granted.

The biggest lesson and greatest thing I ever received from foster care was love. Yes, not all of Aunt Grace's family embraced the five nappy-headed kids, but she did. You know, I don't ever know if I heard her say "I love you," but somehow that didn't matter after everything was said and done—I knew. She was always there to embrace us and more impor-tantly to me than anything, she was consistent. Consistent and routine parenting is so important and I understand that as a parent today. My siblings and I have acquired an entire new family and set of experiences and friends we could have never gained in our previous environment. I often wonder how we would have turned out if the environment had never changed. I feel a lot of who I am is inherent in my nature, however, I truly believe a lot of what I've become is a direct result of foster care. In my experience, foster care provided the foundation for me to start building my house. Yes, every lesson wasn't learned, but having to not deal with the daily struggle of survival allowed me to grow and enjoy childhood. Enjoy learning things and evaluating new circumstances without being overwhelmed by old ones.

I want to end with emphasizing one point to all children who go through foster care. Remember, you are so much more than what you came from. You cannot choose your parents or cannot explain their behavior. You now have the opportunity to really understand who you are and what you can be. An environment will have an impact on what's around it, but you can still rise above it. Think of the flower that never gets watered, the car that's never maintained, the child that is not loved and cared for. All will have negative consequences, if not immediately addressed. Children who are part of the process, keep that in mind as you learn about your new environment. Adults who are responsible for these children, keep that in mind when you have to make that very difficult decision to do what's right for your child. Lastly, for prospective adults who want to truly make a difference in your world, think of what you can do by helping families that don't have the means to care for themselves.

FINDING HOME

By Charisse Nesbit

From the first moment I'd heard of the concept of a foster home as a child, I immediately thought of a place that would be anything but a home. In my mind's eye the only thing the words "foster home" conjured for me was a place with sterile scrubbed floors and large stainless steel sinks big enough for me to crawl my seven-year-old body into and finally be scrubbed completely clean. My siblings and I were gathered in my mother's room, my sister washing my younger brother in a tin pail with stolen water from a neighbor's house, when the idea of us being rescued and taken to one of these mythical places was first introduced to me. The room was filled with discarded clothes, the only light coming from a nearby window. Thankfully it was morning so there was no need to use the oil lanterns that provided our light from night to night. Here we were in the twentieth century, yet we lived as though we were stuck in the 1800's.

My twin brother and I sat on the disheveled unmade bed, waiting for our turn to wash up in the used water. My older brother was nowhere to be found, a common occurrence when he'd managed to stay over a friend's house, escaping the hell our home had become.

"I can't do this anymore, I wish we could just go to a foster home," my sister said, continuing to swipe at my little brother's golden skin with her washcloth.

"Me too," I chimed in, though I didn't even really know what a foster home was. I wasn't even entirely sure I wanted to go. Though it wasn't the most nutritious thing, eating corn chips for dinner and having only occasional adult supervision didn't seem all that bad. We were free, after all. Weren't we?

"I don't know if I want to go," my twin brother said. "We can take care of ourselves. Besides, what would we do there?"

"I don't know, but anything has to be better than this," my sister said, drying off my little brother. I prepared myself for my turn, happy to have something resembling a bath for the first time in what must have been days.

When the lights in our home had been turned off, it was as if time itself ceased to exist as well. I no longer had any idea of time or days as they all seemed unnaturally dark with no interior lights or clocks to guide our way. How we managed to get ourselves up for school every day without an alarm clock or a parent to make sure we went, I'll never know, but we did. I often marvel that I didn't fail the first grade with no one to check my homework or make sure that I did it. My older brother and sister were a big part of that. To this day my sister has her own internal clock that won't allow her to sleep too late. It was more than likely developed during this time. We all developed our own ways of surviving that dark time in our lives, though I'm sure we're not always aware of it.

Though we've managed to fare well in life, those dark days will always be with us in one form or another. Certain memories I have are as clear to me today as the day they happened. For instance, everyone in our neighborhood knew of our situation, and we were often made fun of because of it. One of my neighbors whom I considered a friend, would often taunt me about my situation though her family would occasionally give me food to eat, and milk to drink, though I was allergic. Going to her house was always a bit of a treat though I'd be hesitant to go inside, feeling too dirty and not quite worthy. It was always very clean and smelled of roses. Her father owned a cleaning business, ironically enough, and part of her taunts would be to make fun of how dirty our house often was. Although I was ashamed of how we lived, I never let what anyone else had to say get to me. I still had my pride.

Once, when another neighbor gave me homemade Beefaroni, I didn't eat it all, instead emptying it in a rare clean container at our house and returning her bowl. I didn't want to take the food back to her for fear that she'd think I was not grateful. I didn't know this decision would open me up to yet another taunt. My friend's brother, who happened to be at the neighbor's house when I returned the bowl, remarked, "Of course she brought it back clean," laughing that I'd scraped the bowl of every bit of food since we had nothing else to eat. I never did finish the rest of that food just because of that comment. I actually forgot it in the container until I found it much later when it had grown moldy and I had to throw it out. Still, I would have rather wasted it than to give him the satisfaction of finishing it and having his taunt be true. In spite of my situation and my young age, I still had my pride. I didn't want to give him the satisfaction of eating the food and proving him right, that I was needy. Sometimes I wonder how we survived during those times, but somehow we got through it, until help finally arrived.

I was amazed when the social workers showed up to take us away. I'm not sure how long this occurred after we'd aired our plea in my mother's dark bedroom, but I instinctually knew that someone had heard us and that this woman and man were the people to make our musings a reality. She was young and attractive with rich brown skin and an Indian accent. She wore a professional suit and had straight black bobbed hair. The man was tall and African-American with a nice suit and a strong, straight back. I don't remember much about their introduction to us, but I do remember them saying they would be taking us to a foster home in a place I'd never heard of called Cecilton. It sounded like a huge city to me. I feared being lost in the shuffle of numerous bodies, my name meaning nothing in the throng of people I was sure would fill this place. I was instantly afraid of what would become of my siblings and me.

To my surprise, Cecilton ended up being a town of less than five hundred people without even the one stoplight it has currently. This place was even smaller than where I'd come from! Looking around at the quiet nearly empty streets passing our window as we approached our destination, I began to wonder if this would be better for us after all. When we finally arrived at our new home, I was surprised again to see that a home was exactly what it was. Taking in the small white house with black shutters, I realized my vision of sterile clinical surroundings and stainless steel sinks couldn't have been further from the reality presented to me now. The holly trees in the front yard made it even more inviting, and gave the house the warm feel of Christmas even though it was only October.

Once inside, we were greeted by a small older lady with smooth caramel-colored skin and full round cheeks. She would be our new mother for the next six months until our real mother could find us a new home. Only my oldest brother would stick close to this deadline. Having long taken on the role of man of the house at the tender age of thirteen, he quickly rebelled against the new home with its strict rules and limited freedoms we'd taken for granted while raising ourselves while my mother worked to try and provide for us. He left after about a year, escaping to my grandmother's house, leaving us behind without the little guidance he'd offered to that point.

Our new mother offered us three options in naming her: We could call her Ms. Grace, Mum Grace, or Aunt Grace. We all unanimously chose number three with no discussion necessary. Since we already had an Aunt Grace, the choice was a no-brainer. Besides, Ms. Grace was too formal, and since our mother was still around, there was no one who could replace her, so Mum Grace was not an option. At the time we thought we'd be back with her soon anyway, so there was no need to get comfortable enough to address another woman with any moniker remotely resembling "Mom." We agreed to call her husband "Pop." Mostly because everyone else did already, and having never had a strong consistent father figure around up to that point in my life, there was no memory to worry about replacing.

There were three other children in the home in addition to myself and my five siblings. We split ourselves up between the two rooms upstairs and the two rooms in the fully finished basement downstairs. I was amazed to see two full houses essentially sitting on top of one another. The only basements I'd ever seen at that point were cement holes that were filled with long-forgotten junk. This one had a laundry room, living room, dining room, a bathroom with a tub, and a full kitchen with a bar where we'd eat the majority of our meals.

Hopping onto one of the sparkly red stools which matched the bar and made a cool metallic swishing sound when I turned on them, I spun around in glee as the social worker spoke to my new "aunt." Years later I'd learned from one of the other foster kids at the time that the social worker had told Aunt Grace how "durty dese children are," and that we were badly in need of a bath. It had been relayed to me with the intention to hurt, but at the time, swinging around on my sparkly stool, I was oblivious to the conversation taking place before me. I watched them talking from my spinning sparkly perch, already feeling as though things were looking up. When we'd entered the house we'd seen rows and rows of glass jars holding all kinds of cookies and candy. Aunt Grace had let us choose from them, but did tell us that they were for sale, usually so freebies wouldn't be the norm. It didn't matter. All I knew was that with the candy, the entertaining seating, and the free-flowing electricity, it was already better than where I'd just come from. For now, at least, it was home.

Years later I still remember that first day as clearly as if it had just happened to me. My six-month stay lasted well into my adult life. My mother had married and had us young, delaying her own youth for her late twenties and thirties while we stayed in the foster home. Though she often missed the supervised visits set up at the social services offices, we eventually managed to set up overnight visits at her apartment on our own. We were never adopted at our foster home, and I feel that this was due in great part to our respect for our mother. Though she wasn't around as much as we would have liked, she was still present and at the end of the day, she was our mother.

We'd never live with her again. My sister tried once she'd aged out of the system but it didn't last. Visits on an occasional weekend were fine, but my mother was not ready yet to have us back full time. My sister ended up finding refuge in the army, doing very well and going on to college. She now has a successful career and a family of her own with two very beautiful, bright, well-adjusted children who have the benefit of both their parents being present. My twin brother was fortunate to get a scholarship to private school in the ninth grade. He stuck it out in our foster home until the tenth grade, leaving to my grandmother's house to lessen his commute to school. He also has a beautiful young son who is attending private school and taking advantage of all of the things we'd never gotten a chance to do. He plays soccer, tennis, swims, does karate, and even has a small mini bike that he and my brother ride together on the weekends. My brother is also married with a new son who will also benefit from his father's insight after surviving the system.

My younger brother left our foster home in his early teens to live with my grandmother as well. This was after I'd aged out, but of everyone, I'd stayed the longest. My younger brother has children of his own as well, and a job he enjoys. My older brother is married with three children and is doing very well also. I am the only one of all of my siblings who has yet to have a child of their own. I live in Los Angeles now where I work in film development and still dream of one day becoming a writer full time. Because of my time spent in the system, I want to take my time before deciding on having children of my own. If I do have kids, I want to follow my siblings' examples. While you can't always guarantee things will work out perfectly in the end, I'd like to at least start with both parents being around. Though my older and younger brother have been married and divorced before, they still remain a part of their kids' lives, no matter what. I want to ensure that no matter what happens, I can guarantee the same for any children I may have in the future as well.

While I missed having my biological family around full time as I grew, I have come to understand that I was better off in the system. I'd been fortunate in my experience with foster care. It provided me with free medical care, free dental, and I'd even received a grant from a private organization set up to help foster kids pay their way through college. Because of the school I chose and my status as a ward of the courts, I received the maximum amount of financial aid. This not only paid my tuition in full, but I still had money left over for books. My foster mother sent me my monthly check to pay for my room and board, so overall, I was very well cared for, and I have the system to thank for that. I was also fortunate to still have contact with my biological family, even though I never lived with them again until after I left the system for good. My time in foster care wasn't all roses, and I don't want to give that impression, but I can say definitely that my life would have been very different had it not been for my time in the system. I still keep in touch with the remaining members of my foster family, and to me they're as much a part of my life as my biological family.

I've learned that while it would have been ideal in the minds of most to have grown up in their biological family's home, sometimes home is where you find it. I found mine in a little white house in Cecilton, Maryland.

ALL GROWN UP

By Ryan Thompson
(As told to Charisse Nesbit)

I was just three years old when we first arrived at Aunt Grace's house. I remember when the door opened and I first saw her. I smiled from ear to ear, not aware of how my life was changing or why, and not caring. As the youngest of us five, I didn't know much of what had been going on to bring us to this new place, so I adjusted to our new situation the best. I was completely open to my new "aunt," and to living in a stranger's house. Our mother was always out working to provide for us, so at the time, not having her there didn't impact me much.

As the baby, I was favored and I basked in the attention. I wore what my "Aunt Grace" wanted me to wear with no resistance. To this day, my Head Start picture boasts Aunt Grace's tastes of a checkered jacket with a dark-blue bow tie. Hardly the typical outfit for a child of that age, but I never complained. I was just happy to be taken care of. I ate the foods she prepared with the exception of peas which I often hid in the curve of the bar in the basement where we lived. She doted on me as most people did when I was a baby, and I never argued, never rebelled. I didn't know any other life, and felt there was no other life for me. Aunt Grace was a mother figure to me, and "Pop" was the father figure. He was very quiet but strong, and I admired that silent strength. For a while, living with them was enough and I had no complaints.

As I grew, I began to notice a difference in my situation from the other kids in my neighborhood and the first cracks in my existence began to appear. Though not all of my friends had both parents around, they did have one or at least a blood relative to take care of them, something I didn't. I knew my mother and thanks to Aunt Grace's diligence in keeping us in church, I eventually met up with my father's family during a service. My sister recognized my blood grandfather and sent me up to introduce myself. They recognized me right away and I was welcomed in to their fold, but this was still not enough. Visits to their house were nice, and it was good to reconnect with my father again, but something was still missing.

I missed having parents who were like my friends' parents. Parents who were younger and could do things with me like swim or fish like I experienced when visiting them. Parents who would buy my friends brand-new clothes and not give them Salvation Army specials or hand-me-downs like I got. Both Aunt Grace and Pop were well into their fifties, and coming from a simpler time, fashion wasn't at the top of their list of important things. Also, being older, the most strenuous things they did was to work in the garden, cut grass, clean the house, or go food shopping for Aunt Grace's home business every weekend. I felt like I was missing out on special experiences of my childhood that my friends all got to experience and it began to bother me. What made these kids so special? I was as good as they were; and got good grades like some of them did. Why didn't I have a real family, too?

By the time I hit junior high school age, I began to rebel. My siblings were all leaving the house one by one, and I was left with only my sister Chari. She would soon be leaving to college as well and my last sense of my blood family would be gone. Being young, I didn't yet have the tools to deal with this sense of loss, and I began to rebel. I threw away Aunt Grace's notions of how I should act. I was no longer that obedient four-year-old posing for class pictures in outdated clothes. Instead, I began to hang out with my friends and would even let them come to my house when Aunt Grace was gone, a big no-no in her book. There were other things that went on during those times that she wouldn't have approved of, but I was good at hiding my mischief, and as long as I appeared obedient, she never questioned me.

As the youngest I'd always been able to get away with more than my older siblings, and I used it to my advantage. I guess in a way I was punishing Aunt Grace as well. I'd always been the center of attention though I didn't always want to be. I had a relationship with my father, thanks to Aunt Grace, and this was something my siblings didn't have. Though it helped me feel complete, it caused a divide between them and me. I had something they'd never had, just like I'd always gotten everything. I don't know if we ever really felt the divide, but it was there, and I would do anything to close it and feel closer to them.

They would sometimes come to my grandparents' house with me during special occasions, but they never truly felt a part of my father's family. I'd had more than they ever did, and I felt it made me different. As I eventually found myself alone in Aunt Grace's house once everyone had gone, I decided to try and fill the void that being away from my family had created so long ago.

I eventually moved in with my grandmother, leaving the fold of foster care behind. At the time, I thought I knew better than Aunt Grace. I thought I didn't need her anymore as I felt she was too strict and was keeping me from being the grown man I'd thought I was at the time. Time with her for me had been reduced to chores I had to do and obligations to fulfill. With my grandmother, my responsibilities were more relaxed. The most she'd ask was for me to clean my room which I rarely did. Even when I wouldn't, there wasn't the punishment or consequences that usually came when I was with Aunt Grace. During that time with my grandmother, I felt as though I reconnected with my siblings again. Everyone always came to Grandmom's house for comfort, food, or just because. I could see my siblings again any time I wanted, and in a setting where we weren't always worried about whose turn it was to perform some new chore Aunt Grace seemed to invent daily. We always seemed to be cleaning or cooking or dusting, and now we could simply be—together. I was in heaven.

Being with Grandmom brought our core group of five back together, and solidified our relationship. That bond has only grown stronger through the years, but maybe that would have happened anyway. It's hard to say now. Then, I thought it only happened because I was "home." I was with blood family, and I would never need foster care again. I didn't think at the time that it was necessary for me to have ever stayed with Aunt Grace. I thought I was grown though I was only a teenager. As a teenager, of course I thought I knew everything, but now I know different.

Now I know that the time I spent with Aunt Grace gave me discipline and taught me to be independent. I learned to take care of myself and to be self-reliant, though I would still ask my family for help when times would get tough. As she and Pop grew older, Aunt Grace would let me cook for myself, and wasn't as much the disciplinarian that she'd been when I was younger. After leaving foster care, I went on to graduate from high school and later entered the military. I married young and had children young. I feel this never would have happened had I stayed with Aunt Grace until I aged out of the system. I probably would have gone on to college right after high school and obtained a degree like my siblings, but I've learned that we each have our own path to lead, and I will follow it wherever it takes me with no regrets.

I am very proud of what I have accomplished with my life thus far and the beautiful children I have raised. Because I've had a lot of responsibility early on, I haven't had as much time or money to complete my goal of obtaining a college degree, but it is still a goal for the future. I work in a hospital where I assist daily complicated operations, and I know the procedures almost as well as the doctors. Though I don't aspire to be a doctor, I do one day want to obtain a nursing degree like my mother. Being in the military has allotted me some money for college. But had I stayed in foster care longer, I know I would have come by this money through the resources foster care provided instead of spilling the blood sweat and tears I had to in order to obtain the same goal through the military, but it's all okay. I've learned my lessons my way, and I've grown from each one.

When people now ask me about my childhood, they are often surprised to hear that I was once a foster child. I point out that because I started in the system, it has had nothing but a positive reflection on whom I am today. I point out to them that out of five siblings, four of us have our undergraduate degrees with two also earning masters. I am not limited by being a child of the system, why should I be? None of us were. Facing people who think that foster care is a limitation only makes me work harder to prove them wrong. I've had a lot of responsibilities that took away from me obtaining my degree, but I'm still working on it. After all, who knows what else I can be now that I'm really all grown up?

THEY

By Charisse Nesbit
(For my former neighbors)

They used to laugh when we'd run
With a pitcher of stolen water, back
To the safety of our darkened home.
They used to scold our mother, tsk-tsk,
And shake their heads, all the while...
Turning their backs...

They used to bring the baby in
And wash him up, comb and grease
His soft blond curls into cascading waves,
leaving us dirty, marveling at what a difference
cleanliness made to his glowing yellow skin...

They finally saw the deepness of our plight
And in a move that I hated then,
Picked up the phone, and helped us
In the best way they knew how...
They finally cared.

REPRESENT

REPRESENT

Represent is a magazine for and about foster children published by Youth Communication. Started in 1993 as Foster Care Youth United, it is a bi-monthly magazine that is run by a staff of 30 teens based in New York City. The magazine features essays, poems, and stories, all from the foster care perspective. They give foster care youth a voice, and even help to inform the system and parents on issues and problems the children face, often helping to develop more responsible practices and policies. The voices from the front lines of foster care are varied as the next five stories show. From a boy who finds a father in an unexpected source, to another who discovers how a change of location can make all the difference between success and failure, the stories tell about the foster care experience from the inside, and shows us how we can make a difference on the outside.

FINDING MY FATHER:
MY DREAM DAD TURNED OUT TO BE GAY

BY DOMINICK FREEMAN

I had a fantasy of what I wanted in my dream dad: He would be able to support himself and not be taking me in for the check. He would know how to make money and help me figure out how to have a successful career as an architect. He would understand that my past, which includes being beaten, humiliated, neglected and rejected, was not my fault.

My dream dad would listen and have patience with me. He would love me and respect me and I would love and respect him back. He would be there for me, forever.

Hoping for adoption. I wanted a man in my life, a father figure, because I never had one. My real father left my mother before I was born. According to relatives on my mother's side, he was a gang member who gave me twenty-two other half-brothers and half-sisters.

I desperately wanted to be adopted. But I had been free for adoption since I was eight and my two adoptive placements both failed. At age nine I was supposed to be adopted by a nice guy called Dave, but his other adopted son didn't want me to move in.

When I was ten, my Aunt Sandra and my Uncle Willie, who surrendered me to foster care at age six due to family tension, said they would adopt me, but because they lived in Pennsylvania and I was in foster care in New York, things got complicated and they didn't. My hopes were raised and then smashed. I bounced from one foster home to another. I never stopped hurting.

New Job, Nice Boss

I got a summer clerical job at Bellevue Hospital in Manhattan the summer I was fifteen and went to work for Richard Freeman, the associate director of psychiatry. Richard was a quiet, calm white guy with fewer wrinkles than your average forty-year-old. All the people he worked with talked about how great he was. He turned out to be a great boss, too, because he never yelled at me when I made a mistake.

We left work at the same time, and sometimes, after work, we would hang out and he would buy me ice cream or pizza. This made me even happier to have him as my boss. At the time I met Richard, I was living with a Pentecostal woman in her mid-sixties who devoted all her time to church. She cooked curried goat and white rice with coconut extract and thyme, which I thought was disgusting. A few months after I moved in, I asked her if she allowed kids to swear.

"If you swear at me, I'll send you to another foster home and you'll never come back," she answered. She told me another kid called her a bitch, so she called a social worker on him. Two hours later he left and she never saw him again. For this reason and others, I didn't trust her to become my adoptive mother. I never trusted any of my foster parents. I knew they didn't love me and might disappear any day.

A New View on Religion

My six different placements included a psych ward; a horrible, strict group home; and a home with Mormons who listened to long, boring sermons for six hours every Sunday. The other six days of the week they beat me for little, stupid reasons with rulers, belts, brooms, and a framed picture. Luckily, I didn't get any glass in my skin.

I was glad I left their house after three years because the odds of them beating me to death were two-to-one. I was sick of living with old women and religious people. They couldn't understand my dislike of church and enjoyment of rave music and metal or why I wear black raver pants and a Cradle of Filth shirt. One day I asked Richard, "Do you go to church?"

"Not in many years," he said. I was shocked because everyone I had ever lived with went to church. "Well, what is your view on religion?" I asked.

"To me, church is a place where people are being controlled by fear. I don't feel that it's right for people to impose their religious beliefs on others," he explained. That was the weirdest conversation I had ever had. A grown person shared my opinions! This made me want to draw closer to him.

Bonding on the Subway

Over the summer, Richard and I took the same train home to Brooklyn each night and we got to know each other better. Every day on the train we talked about different political topics: President Bush, the tragedy of September 11th and our corrupt government. We both agreed that we were liberals. That drew us even closer. As our conversations became more personal, I let out my past to him and told him how I had been abused. I told Richard that I was in foster care, that I was not adopted yet, and that I would love to live with a dad, or a mom and dad. I had no idea he was actually listening to me when I talked.

Suspense and Surprise

One day I went into Richard's office and found him looking at an adoption website on his computer.

"Why are you looking for kids who want to be adopted?" I asked. Richard said he was researching the topic of adoption and seeing if he was eligible to be an adoptive parent. This made me really jealous. I wanted to yell, "HELLO? Didn't I tell you that I am free for adoption? Why are you looking at all these other kids when you have me?"

Instead, I just told him, "The kids on there are no bargain, you know."

In the last week of working at Bellevue, Richard and I got ice cream and sat down in Union Square Park. Richard told me about his mother. "Just like you, I had problems with my family. My mother was a person I couldn't stand to be with. I left New York six years ago to go to San Francisco and get as far from her as I could."

That explained why he understood me so well: He had problems with his family, just like I had with mine. Finally I asked him, "Why don't you adopt me?"

"Dominick, I want to tell you something," he said in a real serious manner. "I am gay."

I Want You As My Son

I had chills for a second. I had no idea! He was good-looking and could have any girl he wanted! We had talked about our family relationships but not our romantic relationships, so it never occurred to me he might be gay. I had to think for a minute.

"I don't care that you are gay," I finally told Richard. "I just want you to be a good parent to me. That's what I care about the most."

"I'm not going to make any promises," said Richard. "I don't know how long adoption takes, or all that is involved, but I will try. I hope one day I will have you as my son."

The Secret's Out

The week after I finished my summer job, my social worker, William, asked me if I wanted to bring Richard to a Mets game. When I went to meet Richard at William's office, William walked up close to me, like he wanted to tell me a secret. "I don't know if you know what Richard is doing, but I'll tell you," William whispered. He sounded really, really happy. "He's in the process of adopting you! It's a good thing that you stood up and found a dad all on your own. I'm very proud of you, kid."

I told Richard this and he said, "Well, I was going to keep it a secret, but now you've found out." We laughed throughout the whole game.

No Roaches and No Mice!

The adoption process started in September with a home visit. I loved Richard's apartment. No roaches and no mice! My other homes had a lot of insects, especially water bugs. Richard had already set up my bedroom. I felt so welcomed when his two cats, Sheva and Thelma, wanted all kinds of attention from me. I'd never been to a nice restaurant like the one where he took me, The Second Street Cafe. It was a hell of a good time. What I liked most was that, for the very first time, I got to see how life can be good in New York. Everything was great. This was the right house for me. I wanted to stay as long as I could.

Finally, on May 23, 2003, three days after my sixteenth birthday, my dad became certified as a foster parent and I moved into his house. Almost immediately, we got into a fight over my curfew, which was 5 p.m. None of my friends had to be home that early. We fought about the curfew for weeks.

Then one day, I asked Rich, "If I do what I have to do this month, can I have a later curfew?" He agreed. His acting reasonable made me feel reasonable. For a whole month I came home on time. Richard extended my curfew to 9 p.m. on the weekdays and midnight on the weekends. I was satisfied.

National Adoption Day was a few months later, on November 22, and that was the day Richard and I went to Queens Courthouse to make my adoption legal. I traded my last name of Gonzalez to become "Freeman." Since that moment, I have become a new man.

Bumps in the Road

I feel loved and am happy to be out of the system. I am a free man!

Since my adoption, Richard has proven to be my dream dad, but everything has not gone the way I dreamed. Even before the adoption, there was tension. I had trouble believing anyone would really be there for me in the long run, so I let out a lot of my frustrations on Richard. When Richard told me not to pour ketchup over all my food without asking, or not to interrupt people, I flipped out.

When I decided I didn't want to be on anti-depressants anymore, my dad agreed to let me go off them, but I became much more irritable and slammed doors. I was scared that this adoption could fail like the first two and knew it would end all my hopes of being reunited with the family I was born into. My birth family would never approve of me wanting to be adopted by a man who was white and gay. I tried not to worry so much by reminding myself, "Rich has done more for me and offered me more than everyone in my family put together."

Learning to Change

Richard wants me to be more responsible, and he still lectures me about how important it is to care about the people around you. It has taken me a long time to realize how to be selfless. But I am willing to try because I don't want to be self-centered all my life. Families can't work if each person is only thinking about himself.

I had to be self-centered in the past because it was part of my survival— no one else cared about me but me. But now I realize there is no longer any need to behave the way I used to. I don't have to be anxious about being heard all the time, but can concentrate on listening to others. I'm changing.

A Traditional Family

In the last few months our family has grown. Devon, my dad's boyfriend; and my new brothers, Tyrik, fifteen, and Derrick, eleven, have moved into our four-bedroom house. Derrick, who has a lot of heart and a great sense of humor, is also being adopted by my dad. Tyrik, a foster child who just came into our lives, is also very helpful and supportive. Devon helps us boys with things like cooking and homework and helps keep track of where we all are. I never take my family for granted.

We may not look like a traditional family—we're all guys and all different races—but in lots of ways we are.

I have chores like setting the table, taking out the garbage, and cleaning the bathroom. We go on family vacations to San Francisco, Toronto, Philadelphia, and Boston. Dad takes us away so we can all enjoy different places, but also to advance my education. He has really encouraged my goal to become an architect and is always pointing out differences in city skylines and how buildings are put together. Another difference is I don't have to eat disgusting food. We have food like chicken cutlets, ham and yellow rice—my favorite!

Also, we celebrate traditional holidays. Christmas is to me one of the coolest days. Our TV shows a tape of a fireplace, and we have a Christmas tree and hang ornaments.

Fatherly Advice

I can also talk to my dad about anything, including sex. I love to see how much my dad will put up with at the dinner table when I ask him raunchy questions about fantasies or fetishes, but I can also ask him about serious things like love. One time I was in a bad relationship with a girl and depressed because I felt she was controlling my life. At first my dad laughed, but I told him that was very hurtful.

He stopped laughing and said he had been in a similar relationship once and that no one deserves to be manipulated and yelled at. He told me to wait to speak to her until I was calm and to tell her how I felt. His advice helped me handle a situation that could have escalated. My dad is open-minded and sensitive to other people's problems.

Dreams Do Come True

My GPA is about 88 and I have already been accepted into City College. I want to be as successful as Richard. Because he's been my dream dad, in return I want to give him a dream son. Knowing that he will always be there for me, every day makes me want to make him proud every day, for the rest of his life. I want to be successful, social, and cooperative. For a long time, I was a hermit, but now I'm feeling a lot more communicative.

The love he has shown me has also changed my opinions of gay people. When I was little, being called a "gaylord" or a "faggot" was a real bad thing. In care I heard all kinds of negative things about gay people. I was in this group home from ages twelve to fourteen, and because I was physically and emotionally weak, the boys there questioned my sexuality and made me feel ashamed that I knew gay people. But living with my dad has made me much more open-minded and tolerant.

Being gay doesn't make you a good or bad parent. I think what makes you a bad parent is a lack of compassion, and my dad has lots of compassion. I've only told some of my friends that my dad is gay, because some of my friends assume that gay men molest kids. It offends me when people's heads are in the gutter. I hope that people will change their way of thinking about gays in general.

For people who think that gay people shouldn't adopt, I have to tell you this: I've been way better off having a gay parent in my life than having two straight, abusive parents! I needed a good parent, and I got one.

LEARNING TO LOVE AGAIN
I'VE FINALLY FOUND A FOSTER MOM
I CAN TRUST

BY AQUELLAH MAHDI

The first time Yolanda saw my twin sister, Taheerah, and me, we were cursing out our foster parent. Yolanda was going to be our next foster mom. Who knows what she had in her head about us. We were new to the agency, so the only things in our file were bad things: we violated curfew, and didn't do our chores, I smoked and my sister liked to drink. I believed she thought, "As soon as they act up once, they're out of my home." That was the kind of attitude my sister and I had encountered at the other homes where we'd been.

From One Bad Home to Another

Taheerah and I entered care four years ago, after we told about being sexually abused by our father. The first year we lived with five different foster families. We lived with a woman who only seemed to care about how much money she was going to get for us. Another foster mother's main concern was that we wouldn't say anything bad about her home, which was sweet on the outside but salty on the inside. Those bad experiences made me think all foster moms were the same. I couldn't imagine trusting any of them.

It was a relief when we were placed in a group home, but it hurt not to have anyone looking out for us. We ran free like little animals without an owner to watch us. Three years later ACS closed the group home and we went back to bouncing from one foster home to another.

She Wasn't a Fake

At the agency a few days before we moved into her home, the only thing Yolanda said was, "There are chores and a curfew." I didn't know what to think of her, only that she was going to be my next victim. I was going to try to hurt her before she got rid of my sister and me. I thought it would be better to get kicked out for bad behavior than to have her reject us.

My sister and I walked into Yolanda's home feeling sure that within the next month or two we would be on our way out. There was no need to get all attached to the room, the bed, or even the rules.

But that first day at Yolanda's home my rabbit died. I started to cry. That rabbit was so small and defenseless. It needed me and I let it die. Then Yolanda hugged me. "If that happened to my cat Jackie I would feel the same way that you do," she said. She wanted my rabbit to be buried and offered to buy me another one. That's how I realized she wasn't a fake.

I felt different at that moment. It was like she felt the anger that I had inside of me, and was saying that it was okay to feel that way. That it was okay to be sad and for me to let my guard down, that not everyone in the world was out to harm my sister or me. That it was okay to let someone into my world and let them help me. It was just a hug, but it meant so much.

Feeling More at Ease

As the months passed, I began to feel a little bit more at ease. But memories of my past started to rise to the surface. I started having a lot of bad dreams about my dad, and I got so confused and scared.

One day when I was feeling depressed, I told Yolanda I was feeling sad. She said, "Why do you think that you are sad?"

"I don't know," I replied. "I just do." Then I looked at her and we sat there and laughed. It was like we both knew that I wanted to talk but I wasn't ready to let it all out. She didn't push me. Instead she told me, "When you're ready to talk, text me on my cell phone." That was fine with me. I liked that.

When I told her about my nightmares, Yolanda stayed with me in my room and tried to comfort me. I talked to her a little, but I couldn't get it all out, so she just let me know that she was there for me.

"Any time you need me, come and knock on my door," she said, unlike other foster moms who just called 9-1-1 to have someone come and get me. When she left I was still a little bit scared, but more at ease.

Talking Out My Fears

Sometimes I talked to her about my dad, and how I was scared that he was going to come back and kill me, or how sometimes I could just feel him touching me, even though the abuse stopped years ago.

Sometimes I'd feel like Yolanda, Taheerah and even our foster sisters had vanished from me, like the night devoured them and left me alone. I started staying up so that I could beat whatever might come and try to hurt my new family. I kept a knife to protect us.

Yolanda had to take that away from me. When she did, she reassured me that she would never let anything happen to my sister or me. For some reason I believed her, I guess because she didn't seem to mind that she had to be there for me in the night. Or if she did, she had the perfect way of hiding it so that I didn't feel like I was bothering her.

She Was There for Me

Then, in November, my sister signed herself into a psychiatric hospital because she was feeling depressed. When I saw her at school, she was going to therapy and I was going home. That afternoon, Yolanda got a phone call from someone at the agency. Taheerah was on her way to a hospital upstate. I couldn't believe it.

"Your sister cut herself," Yolanda told me.

"Is she really going to the hospital?"

"Yes, that is what I was told."

I rushed to the phone to call my law guardian to get Taheerah out, but I couldn't get in contact with her. It didn't occur to me until later that Taheerah wanted to be in the hospital.

That still didn't stop me from becoming stressed out. For months, I pretty much stopped eating. Yolanda was there with me during everything.

"Aquellah, I know that you are stressed but you have to eat or you will get so sick," she told me.

"I miss her, I want my sister."

"I don't know why she wanted to hurt herself like that, but I guess that she needed help and she is going to get it now at the hospital," Yolanda told me. She hugged me and I stayed like that, crying on her shoulder for a little while.

I Didn't Have to Worry Anymore

A few nights after that I woke up in a panic. I couldn't stay asleep. Yolanda came into my room. "Aquellah, what's wrong?" I couldn't even tell her how I felt. I couldn't get the words out to say what the matter was.

"Aquellah, you're safe here, okay? If anyone tries to get through the door to hurt you, I will get them." I was glad that she was so aggressive—it made me feel like I could loosen up and let someone else protect me. I didn't have to worry anymore.

I'm grateful to have Yolanda as a foster parent, because in a way she is more than a foster parent; she's a lifesaver. When she tells me (and sometimes she has to tell me this over and over), "You have to stop being the victim," I don't mind. She wants to go with me on my journeys and to help me find my way back home—to her home.

I would love to stay with Yolanda until I age out. She has accepted me, my sister and all the baggage we brought to her home. Instead of pushing us away, she's taught herself how to help us deal with our problems, and whatever we might face in the future.

GREAT EXPECTATIONS:
I PICTURED MY NEW LIFE AS A DOUBLE CHOCOLATE OREO WITH A GLASS OF MILK

By Hattie Rice

When I move to new placements I usually don't have any expectations, but a year ago I moved to a new foster home and I had a fantasy image in my mind. I pictured my new life as a double chocolate Oreo cookie with a glass of milk but instead I ended up with a turkey burger (good and good for ya, but it just ain't the beef).

At the time I was a junior in high school and was living in a group home. When I was told I had to move, I was determined to find a foster mom who could help me get into college, because I knew my books could take me to a better life.

A Dream Foster Mom?

When I met Diane, she seemed like what I was looking for. Diane has a good education; a bachelor's degree and a master's in nursing. She has several jobs: she works as a psychiatric nurse, an editor for a black television station (even though she's white), and has a side hustle in real estate.

Diane is caring, considerate and sacrificing. She's also systematic, sometimes reminding me of Robocop. She plans everything out (kind of scary) and always thinks that she is right (we all do, but she's extreme).

My Hopes Rose

During the long process of getting to know Diane before I moved in, my hopes rose. She started our first chat by asking about the basics, like my hobbies, relationship with family, interest in going to college and the career I might enjoy. (Doesn't she sound like a social worker?)

I probed her to find out her reasons for wanting foster kids, and she told me that she could not have kids but wanted to adopt two girls and create a family. She also said she'd had a rocky relationship with her own mother.

Not in it for the Money

Diane and I continued our conversation during a lunch date at an Italian restaurant (I love a good sausage.) Soon after, we met with another foster youth, Nef, a teen, who was considering moving in, too.

At the Olive Garden by forty-deuce, the three of us talked about what we could expect while living together. When it came to the budget, Diane said, "With the money I receive for y'all, we will figure out a budget. The money you need each month will go in a checking account, and the rest will go in a savings account."

"Whaat! Come one more again?" I yelled. I must admit that even a cynical character like me was impressed that she was disproving the myth that all foster parents only want the money.

Building a New Family

Soon Nef and I stayed at Diane's house for a weekend. I made my cooking debut: turkey burgers, sweet potato fries, and grilled vegetables, which may sound weird but was on point. Afterward Diane showed us how to play Backgammon and Scrabble. I won twice in Backgammon (that was not beginner's luck!) and I lost by one in Scrabble (Diane cheated, I know she did.)

In the morning Diane made breakfast and we headed downtown, where she bought us blue Ralph Lauren sheets and matching Tommy Hilfiger accessories. We also picked out paint and a rug for our new MTV-style crib.

So you can see how, by the time I moved in last summer, I had built a fantasy image in my head of what it was going to be like. I imagined that in our life together I'd be the black Marsha; Nef would be Cindy, the little girl, since she was cute; and Diane would be the *Brady Bunch* father because he knew the answer to every problem, which was annoying during the show but handy in real life. Somehow I forgot that starting any new family from scratch is going to come with misunderstandings.

The Trouble Starts

Once Nef and I moved in, things got complicated. Nef dropped out of summer school after getting jaw surgery and they constantly argued about it. Diane wanted her to do something with her summer, or at least get out the house instead of sitting around watching TV. But who wants to go outside and end up looking like Wesley Snipes? You know black people—you don't see us till after six o'clock.

Diane also decided we were moving five blocks because she wanted to buy an apartment. That infuriated me—I'd already moved three times that year. The move was very stressful, and I felt Diane took it out on us, like she also believed we should be *Brady Bunch*-perfect.

When we were painting my new room, I said I wanted to paint some edging burgundy and the rest tan. "Regular people do not do that," Diane replied. You cannot imagine how tight I was. I felt like she was ridiculing me because of my unfortunate beginnings.

I felt the same way when she seemed more interested in showing me her culture—setting the table right and going to ballet—than learning about mine. She can't watch 50 Cent's *Get Rich or Die Tryin'*? Or at least Dave Chappelle's *Block Party*? That had a French director!

A Puppet on a String

Around Diane, I sometimes felt like I was supposed to act like a puppet following her command. She expected me to do my chores on her schedule, and flipped on me if I was late for school just once. I wanted to tell her, "I had to be a sole survivor just to get by. I don't need you telling me how to do every task."

Even though I had my issues with Diane, I kept quiet while she and

Nef argued. Usually I don't get in arguments because I try to stay detached—not let anyone bother me, not face reality, and keep any anger I feel under control.

Laying back was something I learned as a child, because getting upset with my mentally ill parents only hurt their feelings and never resulted in any change. It was easier to detach from the situation than get my hopes up and then get let down.

But as Diane got agitated, it seemed like she was yelling at me for the simplest things. The tension was getting on my nerves, and I also began to take it personally. I think my feelings got hurt and I got angry because I actually cared about making our relationship work. I figured that I had to be willing to get emotionally involved, whether with love or anger.

"We Have to Make a Change"

One day I decided to jump in when she and Nef were already going at it. (I had the best timing, right?) Diane began to get on me about budgets and my complaints about therapy. I screamed, "I went, okay? Who goes to therapy on their birthday?" In my head I was waiting for her comeback because I was in shutdown mode.

Then she changed the subject, saying that I never told her I was spending the weekend with my best friend. "Either you have a bad memory or I live in an imaginary world," I said.

She picked me shooting a hoop with the Looney Tunes.

I snickered. "Denial is a disease."

She claimed my imagination runs away with me.

I yelled, "Your memory is running away from you and you need to find it." In Elmer Fudd's voice, I added, "Which way did it go? Which way did it go?"

By then Diane was furious, too, and basically said that we could get the hell out of her house.

I said, "We have to make a change."

She had the nerve to answer that she was not changing for anyone because this was the way she was when we came and the way she'd be if we decided to leave.

Tired of Changing Myself

That really hurt me. I often have the feeling that I try so hard to make things work, constantly conforming my beliefs and desires to others, while others don't seem willing to do the same. As a child I didn't go to school because I felt I had to meet the needs of my mentally ill mother. In my group home I never talked about my problems to the social worker, not because I didn't have any, but because I felt the other girls needed her more.

Although it was a different situation with Diane, I felt similarly: I'm going to ballets but you can't see Fifty get shot nine times? I'm crying and all you can say is, "I don't care about your feelings right now." I'm tired of having to change myself and take on responsibility that shouldn't fall on me.

A Mini Mid-Life Crisis

Suddenly, I felt toward Diane like I did with my mother: used, pushed to the limit and unappreciated. I felt like I'd done all I could and she didn't see how hard I tried. Seeing our relationship start to crumble despite my efforts caused me a mean, mini mid-life crisis.

After the argument, I laughed, not because I found it humorous but because my intuition told me the situation would go bad. I felt sad but didn't want to show it. My laugh signified nervousness. I was nervous that living with Diane would not work out and I'd have to find a series of places to live, giving less of myself each move.

Expressing Myself

Our social worker recommended family therapy. To me, it was a waste of time. Nef and Diane argued and seemed to ignore the therapist's advice as if she wasn't conducting the sessions. Even if they spoke calmly, their faces showed the opposite. During the sessions, I was more spaced out than Buzz Lightyear.

But one night we had a heart-to-heart. I was open with Diane. I told her how I felt under-appreciated because she criticizes me. (Hello, I've had more than enough of that! And I already have low self-esteem.) I also said I was feeling alienated because some tiny remote part of my heart (when I say tiny, I mean smaller than Michael Jackson's nose) cared for them and didn't want us to be so angry at each other.

After the discussion I felt relieved, not because I believed things were going to get better, but because I was able to express my feelings rather than keep everything bottled up inside.

Calm and Serene

The next day when I got to therapy everybody I'd ever met at the agency was there. They told me they'd decided Nef should leave the home. I think all three of us were shocked. We went the rest of the week without arguing, making the best of our last week together. She started packing while Diane and I prepared for our new life, only the two of us.

Nef moved out on a Sunday. When I walked her out, I felt happy to see her go someplace where she might feel more comfortable, but also scared because this was the moment of truth for Diane and me. And you know what? Since then we've had no major arguments, just little discussions about the budget sheets and chores. My emotions, which were once like an Oklahoma twister, now feel calm and serene.

Bringing Up Past Feelings

Looking back, I think some of my anger toward Diane was simply my feelings about my mom spilling out because I've never confronted my family with how they made me feel down and depressed. Instead, I tried to ignore my feelings. But when I confronted Diane, I was probably taking all the anger of my childhood out on her.

I've also realized that it's time for me to let go of my technique of staying detached. For years that technique allowed me to not let anyone's feelings disturb my composure, but it's become a problem for me that I'm constantly hiding behind my shield of security. To get close to Diane, I've had to make the transition to actually caring, and as weird as it may sound, that's a really big step for me.

Good-bye Baggage

Even though this adjustment has made me so uncomfortable, slowly I see that I'm getting more comfortable. Ever since I entered foster care at fourteen, I've kept a big box full of bags in my room in case I needed to move out. I never expected to have a home or to feel stable.

But one day Diane politely asked me, "Could you clean out that big box in your room?" Inside I was hollering, *No! No! No!* But surprisingly, I decided to rid myself of all that extra baggage. It helped that I had Remy Ma's "Conceited" playing in the background to boost me up. (The music was intentional.) I felt safe and secure throwing those bags away, confident about where I was in my life and proud that I'm trying not to let my past experiences control my life.

Reprinted from *Represent*, Copyright 2006, with permission from Youth Communication/ New York Center. (www.youthcomm.org)

GOODBYE, HARLEM:
I MIGHT HAVE BEEN A HUSTLER IF I WASN'T SHOWN ANOTHER WAY

By Antwaun Garcia

I met my boy when I was eight. He was shy and something of a follower, but cool. If I cut school, he would cut with me. If I went to the candy store, he'd buy candy if he had money or he would take it.

My boy was growing up a lot like me—on the streets all times of the night, not wanting to go home. Some days his father would hit him, or my boy and his siblings wouldn't eat, because even when their moms was sober and wanted to cook, she couldn't afford food. We became Robin Hoods, stealing from the Bravo store to feed the poor.

Stealing to Eat

I wasn't thrilled about stealing to eat, but it was so easy to do it became a habit. We would walk in the store and act like family, yelling, "Mommy wanted this!" Or, "Moms needed bread for sandwiches in the morning." He would put a few items under his shirt.

I would walk out first and wait for the "walk" sign. As soon as the light changed, I would open the door and he would run right through and across the street into my building.

We had tons of fun together, playing sports, chilling on the park benches eating stolen food, and laughing it all off. Even though our situation wasn't good, we found ways to enjoy life.

But when I was ten, I went into foster care and moved to Queens with my aunt. Moving to Queens was so unexpected I didn't have a chance to say good-bye to him or any of my friends. Later, I wondered about him and all my family. I missed being home and wondered how they were holding up.

A New World

When I arrived in Queens, I felt very weird. My aunt lived in a housing development with security and, between each group of four buildings, a huge circle of flowers and sprinklers. I'd never seen flowers like that in Harlem. Maybe once in a blue you would see some dude selling roses on a street corner, rolling to your window and saying, "Flowers, flowers for your loved one." But that was it. In Queens, I felt like Dorothy in *The Wizard of Oz*. I clicked my shoes three times and I was in paradise.

Still, adapting to my new home was really difficult. My aunt had rules like, "Be home at dark." I thought, "What the f-ck? Home by dark?" I was used to coming home at midnight.

I also had to do chores and homework, be in bed by nine, and attend school daily, which was new for me. I hated it from the jump.

Keeping Up My Game

The biggest change was emotional. Even though I was safe, I always had this feeling that someone was going to double-cross me and I stayed cautious, my hands ready to swing. I didn't know how to react to courtesies, like someone holding doors for me or saying, "Good morning, have a nice day!" I was like, "Uh, duh...okay! Whatever!"

In Harlem, people weren't nice to me unless they knew me or my relatives. It took me a while to realize that, surprisingly, the nice people in Queens didn't have a hidden agenda.

I also found myself acting like I was back in the ghetto even though I had everything I needed. I'd steal food from stores when I had food in the house, or sell weed and bootleg CDs to make some money even though I didn't need to. I couldn't seem to get hustling out of my system. I still enjoyed the thrill and excitement of possibly getting caught, and I didn't want to lose my game. I never knew if I'd end up back in Harlem again, taking care of myself.

I Could Make It

Living with my aunt, I also felt isolated. I felt I couldn't trust anyone and had no one to really talk to. My aunt's family acted stubborn and proud, and made fun of each other for being dumb or making mistakes. I feared they thought they were too good for me. I never felt comfortable enough around them to tell them what I felt, so I kept to myself.

The older I became, the colder my heart became. For years, I isolated myself from all of my family. I barely went back to Harlem to see my extended family or my old friends. I missed my mother and father, but I was also angry at them for letting me end up in care and for being out of touch for long periods of time.

Instead, I kept my head down and tried to take what Queens offered me. In school, I finally learned to read and write. I became a writer here at *Represent* during high school, earned my diploma, started an associate's degree and began to believe I might make it as a journalist or working in the music industry. Slowly, I began to see myself not as a kid who would need to hustle his way through life, but as someone who could make it.

Back on the Block

When I was in high school, I started feeling comfortable taking the train back to Harlem. One afternoon when I was eighteen, I saw my boy and his fam. As I approached him and his uncle on the steps of his building, they said, "Oh, shit, yo, that's Twaun. What's good, son?"

They sounded excited to see me, but the way my boy paved greeting to me was funny. He gave me a fake pound, a quick slap, like, "Don't touch my hand." At first I didn't pay any mind to it. I was happy to see my people.

We started talking about what had been going on in the 'hood since I left. It was the same sad violin story: a couple of people locked up, some shot, some on crack, and a bunch either in foster care or dead. I kept my head down for a moment thinking about what they went through. It hurt.

We were quiet for a moment looking around the block. I asked my boy, "What you been up to, fam?" He said, "Nothing. Same old shit, different day."

"This Nigga Changed"

I started telling him that I'd just achieved my high school diploma and planned to go to college, and that I wrote for this magazine, trying to make big moves.

Judging by his facial expression, he wasn't too thrilled to hear I was becoming successful. I noticed his posture changed and his tone got more serious. He eyed my fresh gear, my lion-piece chain, the three rings on my fingers, and the earrings that were shining more than 42nd Street at night. I guess he assumed I was caked up.

Then he tried to clown me in front of his brother and uncle, saying, "Oh word, so you doing your thang." He laughed like my goals in life were something humorous to him, like I was some stuck-up punk from the suburbs who wasn't 'hood enough to be back home.

He took another pull of his cancer stick and told his uncle, "Yo, this ain't the same little kid I know. This nigga changed."

Then he got in my face and said, "You pussy! You ain't the same cold-hearted young nigga who used to be real and hold shit down."

My Boy Threw Hands

At first I thought he was joking, but he wasn't. His eyes were squinty and his cheek muscles were tight. I was caught off guard. I never thought my boy would attack my character or throw hands with me. I thought he would be happy to see me doing my thang.

I wanted to fix his lip. I was thinking, "We'll see how much I changed when I punch you in your mouth." I am a quick-tempered dude but I fell back and kept my cool. Instead of applying physical force, I played the mental game.

I replied, "So what makes me different? Because now I have a little money in my pockets? Or because you still that same cat hustling for years with no bread, struggling to make ends meet, and still eating off your mom's welfare check?"

He got upset, and I could tell his family didn't like my comment, either. His younger brother started to ball his fist as if to swing at me. But I continued, "Is it because you're still that same punk who needed me to fight your battles, take groceries from the store because your moms couldn't afford them?"

His uncle started cursing at me at the top of his lungs. "What! Who the f-ck are you to disrespect our family!" He wouldn't stop, saying every curse word in the book.

Saying Good-bye

As soon as I began taking my coat off, preparing for someone to pop off, their moms came out. I felt bad for making that comment about her because she looked very ill and was coughing. She yelled, "Antwaun!" and gave me a hug and a kiss on the cheek. "Boy, I haven't seen you since you was that little angry, always-fighting, peasy-headed kid, and now look at ya, you full grown and handsome."

I smirked while saying, "Thank you." She began telling me how hard it's been, especially since she'd been diagnosed with breast cancer. I could see the coldness in her brown eyes and hear the pain in her voice.

I felt for her. She was always cool with me. When her kids ate, I ate, too. When I wanted to get away from my house, she always said I could come through. She was funny and smart, just not smart about getting caught in the crack game.

Then the uncle came into our convo and told her that I wasn't allowed around here no more. I gave him a cold look as my teeth scraped each other like nails scraping the blackboard. I said, "Say no more!" I gave their mother a kiss on the cheek and said it was nice to see her after so many years. She replied, "The same with you, Antwaun. I am so proud of you!"

Not the Same Kid Anymore

As I walked away, I felt upset that I had lost my boy who I had been cool with for years. Thinking it over, I realized that he wasn't jealous of me because of what I was wearing, but because of the goals and dreams I believed were possible.

He had stayed behind in Harlem, and his Harlem had been what it was for me: crack, poverty, drugs, 5-0 and violence. Could I expect any more from him than to live up to his environment? Could I expect him to be happy for my good fortune when he wished to have the opportunities I was given? Don't get it twisted, I was not being cocky, but realizing I've been fortunate.

In Queens I'd gotten the chance to start a whole new life, including going to school and living in a positive environment where I felt the freedom to become more than a punk. He was stuck living a lifestyle that he didn't choose.

Moving On Up?

In the last few years, I've thought a lot about that last convo with my boy. As I get closer to aging out, it seems like I might end up moving back to Harlem. That feels weird, like I could wind up right back where I started, even though I've worked hard to be moving on up, as they said on *The Jeffersons*.

I wonder, "When I age out, will I become the educated and professional person I hope to be, or will I just go backwards?" I fear that, no matter how much success I may obtain, I could always fail at any moment.

What my boy couldn't see is that I still battle my own inner demons. I still carry around a 'hood mentality that makes doubt I'll reach my dreams. Despite the hopeful picture I painted for my boy, it's hard for me to believe that long-term goals, like finishing college, will be things I'll live to achieve.

I often ask the people close to me, "Can I make it?" With reassurance from other people, I've started believing in myself, but it hasn't been easy. I'm not like many of the people I know from Queens or in college, who seem so confident of their futures.

But at least I know that hustling can never be a route to a good life. That right there should keep me on the straight path, safe from ever becoming the worst parts of the Harlem I grew up in.

ME VS. THE WORLD
WHAT HELPED ME GET THROUGH COLLEGE? RAPPING, AND TWO MENTORS WHO BELIEVED IN ME

By Joseph Alvarez

It was time to go. My stuff was all packed up in the back of the truck. My staff members, Sue and Randy, were ready to pull off. But, damn, I didn't want to leave. "Why can't I stop looking at this old-ass house?" I thought.

Bill, one of the group-home staff, was standing in the driveway, and some kids were sticking their heads out the window. I felt like they were staring at a ghost.

I was usually the one giving "words of wisdom" to the other kids, telling them, "Never get used to this shit, the group home is not forever!" Now I found myself wanting to hold on to the group home like a motherless infant. Why was I feeling scared, abandoned, lonely?

Off to College!

"Joey," Bill said in a joking way, "are you ready, man?"

I laughed and said, "Yeah...Yeah, I'm ready, dog." Playfully pretending to punch me, he said, "Knock 'em dead, man!" He gave me a hug and that was it. *SLAM!* I shut the car door and I was off to college! Life after the system had officially begun.

"Man, me going off to college? This can't be happening. Kids like me don't make it this far," I thought, feeling excitement and fear as we drove toward Manhattan. It was forty-five minutes but felt like forty days and forty nights.

After eight long spiraling years in care, I was on my own with $3,000 I had saved up from my summer job. I felt rich and free and sure of myself. I knew I was going to make it!

Would I Make It?

"Damn, this is an ugly building," I thought. The car had stopped in front of my dorm at the School of Visual Arts in downtown Manhattan, where I was to study film editing. The place looked worse than the group home! I checked in and began unpacking my stuff. As Randy handed me the last of my things, I knew it was me versus the world.

We parted ways with hugs and words of encouragement. Then it was just me, my stuff, and my feelings of uncertainty. I almost felt like the walls of the small room were closing in on me. Only God knew how scared I really was that day.

When I first came to the group home at ten years old, I hated myself, the people around me, and anybody who tried to help. I felt the world had already killed my parents and my grandma, and I was going to be the next to die.

A Walking Time Bomb

For the next four years, I was a walking time bomb. Even if you didn't cross me, you were going to get it! Why? Because fighting was my way of showing the world how helpless and hurt I felt inside. How else does a young boy cope when everything he ever loved gets snatched from his heart?

By the time I was fourteen, most of the staff and social workers had checked me off as a kid who would amount to nothing—except one staff. Hobin was one of the coolest guys you'll ever meet. He was also an ex-crackhead and former alcoholic, so let's just say he had a sixth sense for detecting somebody trying to get over.

One night I came in the house real late and as high as the bright moon in the sky. I was trying to play it cool. At the front door, I thought, "I wonder if he saw the headlights from the car dropping me off? Ahhhh, fuck it, Hobin's probably in the office watching TV."

"Step in the Office"

As I opened the door, I saw big ol' Hobin standing right there waiting for me. I knew I was in deep trouble for coming home high as a cross-eyed eagle.

"You had fun," Hobin said in his deep voice.

"Yeah, it was cool," I said, doing my best to avoid eye contact.

I guess the smell of a marijuana forest gave me away, because as I was heading up the stairs, Hobin leaned in to smell me.

"Step in the office," he said in a harsh tone. Then he grabbed me by the shirt and pulled me close to him and let me have it. "What the f-ck? I told you about coming in this house high? Are you fucking stupid? You want to be a fucking crackhead? You want to be a fucking bum? You have something that most people don't have—intelligence! Take it from me— you keep getting high you are going to be a fucking junkie! Now go upstairs and go to sleep and don't you ever let me see you come in this house like that again!"

A Staff who Believed in Me!

Some may say that it wasn't right for Hobin to grab me like that, but I say that some people in the system don't seem to give two shits about us kids, and Hobin was one of the rare staff who did. He never abused us, but kept it real and pure, never sugarcoating the truth. He was rough, but he believed in me and always said I had a gleam in my eye.

After that day, I wanted to prove that Hobin was right about me. I was not going to be like my drug-addicted parents. I was smart and would make it.

As I started doing better in school and checked my behavior, I liked the feeling I got hearing people talk positively about me, like, "Joey's doing good," or, "You from a group home? You don't act like it." I got a thrill from changing people's minds about how group-home kids act or look.

Those comments fueled my determination not to follow the book of my life that my parents wrote: "How to Be a F-ck Up." I had made up my mind to write my own chapters in my own book of my life.

Growing up poor teaches you one of two things: either you become a compulsive spender when you have money, or you become a tight budgeter. I sometimes wonder if I should have gone to college for accounting, since I can stretch $5 to last a week.

I Wanted to Drop Out

But during my first year of college, my bank account was dwindling along with my hope and confidence. At times I would call the group home to say what's up and I'd get a strange feeling, like the people at the end of the line didn't want to know me anymore and everybody was abandoning me. After a while I stopped calling.

I became a loner and kept to myself at college because I couldn't relate to the kids there. It was a private art school, and most of the students were rich and preppy. They seemed to have no idea how to relate to kids like me, and I had no idea how to relate to them.

One typical time I was in my dorm and I overheard one kid say to another, "I was so pissed off at my mom 'cause she wouldn't let me hold the credit card!" I thought to myself, "If that's the worst of your problems, let's trade lives!"

I would have dropped out of college during my first year if it wasn't for my mentor, Jennifer.

My Mentor Pushed Me

I'd call her, saying, "Look, Jen, I feel like I'm wasting my time in this school. I would be much better off getting a job and living in my own apartment."

"Yeah, okay, Joe. You think a minimum wage job is the way to live? You got to be fucking kidding me! You're way too smart for that kind of life. Now call your advisor and sign up for the next semester!" she'd tell me.

She had more belief in me than I had in myself. We had the same conversation semester after semester until I got so close to graduating that I was only a few steps away from reaching my goal.

But for a long time, I believed people at my school looked at me as an outsider. I knew I had to change this. The only way I was going to feel good about myself was to find a way to fit in.

One day my college was having a dance. I forced myself to go, telling myself that I was going to be fine. The music was loud, people were dancing. I had found the couple of friends I'd made. Then the DJ announced to the crowd, "Yo! Listen up! We having an open mike in five minutes."

I thought, "I'm a go up there and tear that shit up, let all these fucking funny kids know who's the best."

"You ready?" the DJ asked. I was nervous as hell, but I grabbed the mike. I'm not sure what I said, but I had been rapping for years and had a confident swagger. People were staring at me like, "Where did this kid come from?"

When I was done, people came up and told me how good I was. Damn, I was feeling good.

Music Helped Me Connect

For weeks after that, random people would come up to me and mention the open mike, like, "Hey, man, you pretty good at rapping." Every time there was a freestyle or anything having to do with music, they would call me. I finally started to feel comfortable at my school.

When I started making music and writing songs, it was as if I had learned a new language and the people that I once could not communicate with understood my new tongue. Instead of being the anti-social kid, I became the kid that others wanted to be around. If they had raps or were singers, they knew I was the man with the music. As I got more involved, I began to feel like part of something and less alone.

Comfortable with our Differences

Through music, I also met two guys who became my good friends,

Sulton and Razi. Other than our interest in music we were like night and day. Sulton and Razi both came from middle-class backgrounds, but they never judged me for being poor. Instead, they seemed to respect me for managing to conquer my crazy life.

Over time, we became comfortable with our differences. I realized I didn't have to have the same background as somebody for us to get along.

College never did get easy, but as time went by I learned how to handle the tremendous stress. I worked, stayed focused on school, hung out with my friends and, eventually, made it through.

On graduation day I had only $20 in my pocket but I felt like a million bucks. My sister Melissa, my guidance counselor, and my ex-girlfriend were all there. The graduation was at Lincoln Center (the world-renowned music center) where everything was real proper. I had on a collared blue shirt with some nice slacks and spit-shined shoes.

It seemed like another four years passed during the graduation ceremony. Just when I thought they would finally announce the class of 2002, someone would give another speech.

"A Success Story"

Finally the main speaker finished his long "I want to save the world" speech and said the words I wanted to hear: "May the class of 2004 please rise."

Oh boy, I was so eager to take that walk across the stage, shake the funny-looking white dude's hand and do backflips down to my seat. But when my name was finally called, I got real serious with a straight face.

As I received my degree, I thought about how hard I had worked to get there. I felt that I was what they call "a success story." I wanted to say to everybody who hadn't believed in me, "Look what I did! And you thought I couldn't do it! Ha!" Then I faced the crowd and pumped my degree in the air.

OTHER VOICES

OTHER VOICES

There are many other stories of foster care to be told. These include those who have gone through the system themselves, as well as others affected by the system through parents who took in foster children. These are the stories rarely told in the media. Stories of love and struggle, caring and understanding. Stories of children who had to share their parents with strangers, and a former foster child who once slept on trains until she found refuge in a group home for young girls where she could finally be safe.

DARICE CLARK

Darice Clark is a writer currently living in Los Angeles. The daughter of a mother who opened her home to foster children, she was exposed to the revolving door of foster care from the age of three to ten. During that time her mother took in between twenty to twenty-five children of varying ages, ethnicities, and personalities. Though she had to share her mother with these "borrowed siblings," she recognized the benefits a stable home provided for kids who may not have had it otherwise. She feels that there is a belief that foster kids have more behavioral problems than other kids, but given a chance and the right environment, they can grow to become healthy and normal. Her essay, "Borrowed Siblings," is the story of four of the many kids who came through her life, and changed it forever.

BORROWED SIBLINGS

By Darice Clark

"Some of these kids are not like other kids," my mother tells me. I am five years old.

"Why not," I say.

"Some of them have parents who need help or can't take care of them yet. So they'll stay with us until their parents can take good care of them."

"What's wrong with the parents?"

"They're too young or, well, are kind of sick and need time to get well. Understand?"

"Yes."

"So as long as they are here, they're our family. Okay?"

"Okay."

"Some of the kids have been hurt, real bad. So sometimes you can not be as rough. I also need you to tell me if they don't play or if they stay quiet for real long."

"How come?"

"I just need to know. It's important. Can I count on you? Are you going to be my big girl?"

"Yes, Mommy. I'm your big girl."

"Good girl."

We sit on my bed in my bedroom, one of four in our house located in the Jamaica neighborhood of Queens, New York. My mother kisses me on the cheek and leaves the room to finish laundry. I go back to playing with my favorite Barbie, the Malibu one.

Even though my parents became foster parents when I was three, the above conversation is my first complete memory of that experience. My parents provided foster care until I was ten years old.

My great-grandparents raised my mother, whose mother had died when she was a toddler. Her father was not in the position to care for her at the time. My mother wanted to give back to children who had been separated from their own parents. I also suspect my mother thought I needed play-mates, since at the time, my two older sisters were basically out of the house. One was living on her own attending college and the other was almost finished with high school when my parents began providing foster care.

Other memories that surface are the visits. There were the visits to "Comforting Arms," the agency where my mom would take my foster sib-lings and me. It gave the birth parents a chance to spend time with their kids and the social workers a chance to assess if the birth parents were ready to take back their children. The birth parents also visited our house with the social workers for the same reasons.

I liked the visits at the agency better. It was easier for me to eavesdrop there. The adults would sit on a couch in a room adjacent to the playroom. All the kids would run around playing but the door would be open so the adults could see and hear all the kids. I just had to wait for someone to throw the inevitable fit or start a fight. I did not even have to be patient because usually one of the boys complied within the first two minutes of a visit, distracting all the adults and giving me my moment to hide behind the couch.

Crouched between the couch and the wall, not moving a muscle, I listened carefully. I learned about all sorts of things like drug rehab, next of kin, teenage parents, wards of the state, custody battles, probation, court dates, and judges. I thought television was interesting. Television had nothing on adults.

This was the seventies, long before cable television gave children such easy access to the world of adults and conversations such as those I now became privy to. Even though I did not understand half of what was being said, I got from the hushed tones that it was serious and a special peek into the mysterious world of grownups. That was reason alone for me to live for my visits to the agency. Escaping was always easy, too, because, again, someone always threw a fit or started a fight toward the end of the visit.

The visits the birth parents made to our house with the social workers were very informative as well. It was always interesting to see what the parents looked like. I developed biases. I liked the teenage parents but not the alcoholics. It was clear to me the teenagers just needed time to grow up. I did not like the alcoholics because some of my uncles and cousins were, and I saw how annoying they were when they were drunk.

Taking in foster kids also created the desire to lose or at least rent out some of my permanent relatives to other families. At age six it made perfect sense to me that I should be able to trade in some of my uncles or cousins. I wanted to swap some of my favorite foster siblings for the relatives I could have easily done without. Like being able to exchange a shirt that does not fit for a new pair of shoes. When I suggested this to my mother, she explained that sort of thing was not possible since the kids had their own families to return to and that over time I would get used to Uncle Ernie. The foster kids left but I never got used to Uncle Ernie. That's another story.

Most of my foster siblings stayed for a few months and then returned to their families while a few would ping-pong back and forth between our home and their families' homes.

Odd thing is I remember loving all of my foster siblings. Even though now I do not remember most of them. We had anywhere from two to six foster kids staying with us at a time. But I was a kid. Since my mom said they were family as long as they were in the house, in my mind and heart they were. I was distraught every time one of them left and thrilled when one returned.

As an adult I wonder how many of them went back to their birth families. How many ended up in other foster homes? Which ones were permanently in foster care? Were they ever able to forgive their birth parents and create a life with them? Where do they live now? Do they remember my family and me? These are questions I live with and will never have answers for.

Though I don't remember them all, there are the four who live in my memory and heart the most.

1. Natasha. The Artist.

Natasha was one of my favorites. Most of the kids who stayed with us were black since my family is black, but Natasha was white. Part Russian, with an angelic head of curly blonde hair, talkative, and round like a teddy bear. When I look back I realize there was an explosive energy about her, like a firecracker waiting to be lit. When I wonder about her from time to time I always imagine she is a famous artist living somewhere exotic. I have this fantasy because she loved using the walls of my house as a canvas for her Crayola masterpieces. Really they were.

It is Natasha's first week in the house. She is four years old and I am seven. I, along with my foster sister Taylor, five, and foster brother Brian, eight, are watching television when Natasha runs into the living room right in front of the television.

"Come see, come see," she says beaming with pride and excitement. Sensing mischief and adventure, the three of us immediately follow. We are not even upset she interrupted our television time. Instinctively we know the disruption will be worth it. Boy, is it ever. Natasha leads us to the upstairs landing. Along the entire stretch of hallway, she has created a crazy, complicated mosaic, not just a patch here or there like other foster siblings have done in the past, but the entire length of hallway wall is covered with a Crayola mural three-and-a-half feet high.

Immediately there is admiration for the audacity of Natasha's act and fear for my mother's rage. Although at that age I did not have those words. My first thoughts were just "Wow" and "Boy, is she in trouble."

I am not alone. Taylor and Brian also stare at the wall in sheer amazement. Then the three of us gently touch Natasha's crayon marks, testing to see if they are real. From there we step back to take in the whole view. We confer on the six-color pattern. We point out details to one another as we admire the work. It is as if we are modern curators at a gallery considering whether or not we will place this new artist's work on our permanent display. Natasha beams and soaks up the adoration with delight.

Then we hear my mother's footsteps. This will not be good. Suddenly I am crushed because I know I will have to help clean the wall. The standard punishment for writing on walls is cleaning them. Natasha will also have the dreaded timeout. I have seen this before. I notice Taylor's and Brian's faces fall as well. They, too, know the drill. Natasha is the only one still full of joy and peace, expecting my mother to have the same reaction we did. She is blissfully ignorant of her impending fate.

My mother actually screams in shock at the sight. Until that moment I am sure she never considered an entire hallway wall, anywhere, let alone one in her own house, being so thoroughly defaced.

"Who did this!" my mother yells. Taylor, Brian, and I step back as far away as possible from Natasha, as though creating physical distance will absolve us of guilt by association.

Natasha, brilliantly assessing the situation, does the most normal thing in the world. "Not me," she replied. Given that the person who speaks first in these situations is almost always the guilty party, my mother pounces.

"Let's see," my mother says as she grabs Natasha's hand and walks her to the wall. Natasha is the shortest out of the three of us. Clearly the artwork reaches as high as Natasha's arm can reach fully stretched out. The cop in my mother emerges. "Natasha, raise your arm."

Conclusive evidence. My mother moves from cop to jury to judge in three seconds flat.

"Natasha, you're in timeout for four minutes. When you're done you'll help them clean the wall." My mother picks Natasha up and takes her downstairs. The three of us follow.

My mother puts Natasha in the timeout chair that faces the corner in the downstairs hall. When you are seated in the chair, you are not allowed to turn around and see what you are missing behind you or the time gets extended. It is sheer torture.

Natasha screams bloody murder and gets out of the chair. My mother puts her back in the chair. This process repeats a few times. Finally, my mother tells Natasha if she ever wants to touch a crayon again, she will sit in that chair and not make one sound while she is in it. Natasha sits. She whimpers but she does not move. It is enough of a compromise for my mother. My mother turns to Taylor, Brian, and me.

"The rest of you will help me get the rags, the buckets, soap, and water."

"But we didn't do anything wrong," I protest. I know this is useless but still I can not stop myself.

"She ruined an entire wall and not one of you said anything. All of you just stood there. Come."

Brian and I both start to protest, create a defense, but my mother's "Do not mess with me now" look on her face stops us. The three of us bow our heads in shame and follow my mother.

By the time we come back with the cleaning supplies Natasha's time-out is over. We all head upstairs with my mother carrying the two filled buckets. Taylor, Brian, and I already have our rags. My mother hands Natasha hers. My mother assigns each of us a section to begin cleaning. We all hesitate. It just seems wrong to erase such wonder.

"What are you all waiting for," my mother barks. "When I get back most, if not all of that wall, better be clean or no one gets dessert tonight. Understand me?"

"Yes, m'aam," Taylor, Brian, and I mumble. Since we are older, we are the only ones expected to answer. Masterpiece or not, I want my Sara Lee pound cake for dessert that night. So I begin cleaning. The rest follow suit.

Natasha would have a few more wall creation episodes throughout her stay but never the length of an entire wall again. The rest of us were on constant watch and managed to catch her mid act before she could do too much damage. Cleaning an entire hallway took forever and killed any desire I might have had to be a graffiti artist. I did not need to repeat the experience. Taylor and Brian felt the same way. So for once we were a united front. Thanks to my mother's use of collective punishment.

Now that I am older I wondered if it had the same effect on Natasha. I hope not. I hope she's some famous graffiti artist or modern painter somewhere wowing critics the world over. After a few months with us she was returned to her birth mother. I never heard about her again.

2. Brian. The Singer.

Brian is a bittersweet memory. He was one of the ones who came and went a few times. He was a year older than me. He was a light-skinned black boy with a sweet and gentle spirit. He was also extremely hyperactive with Attention Deficit Disorder (ADD). So unfortunately he was only still when he slept. He rarely slept.

He was with us because his mother beat him. I could not understand how anyone could beat a child, especially someone as sweet and as loving as Brian. As an adult I can see how a struggling, single mom, with no parenting skills or support would be tempted to beat a child who never stopped moving, talking, or singing. I am in no way excusing the abuse. I just now understand the circumstances.

In the beginning we figured out that if he got someone's complete attention for a few minutes at a time, Brian's yelling and throwing of fits stopped. We basically took turns paying attention to him since his need for it was almost constant. Once he realized he would get someone's attention most of the time he calmed down. But that was not a practical long-term solution. Eventually Brian was placed on the right medication so his activity mellowed to a constant hum in the house. At that point we could treat his behavior like it was a radio with an "off" button that never worked.

Brian was always restless but usually cheerful. Thanks to his ADD he never stayed on one subject or song long enough for me to get bored, so he just became another source of entertainment. Now that I think about it, living with Brian for almost two years is probably one of the reasons I am so patient and rarely ruffled by other people.

Brian's two years with us went that he would be placed with us for a few months, go back to his mom for a few weeks, and return to us for a few months, repeat. I think I was seven when it was the third time that he came back to us. My parents had to actually pick him up from the hospital after him having been with his mom. Brian was bruised black and blue from head to toe. He also had cigarette and iron burn marks on his arms and legs. It was the first and last time I had ever seen child abuse up close. I hope I never see it again.

When I asked my mom how anyone could hurt their own child like that, she said she didn't really know, just that some people can't help it or stop themselves.

"That's why it is good we're a foster family," she said. "Daddy and I do this so kids like Brian have a safe place to be until they have family who can take good care of them."

From that point on I was proud of my parents being foster parents. I also learned at an early age that love really does make a difference. A few weeks later after his return from the hospital, Brian had bounced back. He still had bruises but his spirit was beginning to return.

One day my mother was making lunch for all of us when the song, "My Girl," by The Temptations came on the radio. Brian jumped up and began singing along to the song word for word, serenading my mother. For weeks it was his favorite game. After awhile he did not even need for the song to play on the radio. He would spontaneously burst in to the song and sing its entirety on random occasions whenever my mom walked into the room.

With his love for music and his endless energy, I wonder if he became a musician or rapper. I could see him being a celebrity. Or maybe he became an entrepreneur? Once he was able to channel that energy, I could see him being focused enough to run a business. I hope wherever he went that his sweet nature and love for music was nurtured. Brian eventually was placed with another relative, an uncle I think, and I never heard about him again.

3. Tyrone. Escaped Chicken.

Tyrone came to us when he was three weeks old. I was seven. I still remember his café au lait-colored skin with the reddish tint and how tiny he was as a baby. As a kid his lips were huge. It took a few years for the rest of his face to catch up with them. Everyone loved teasing him about his fat lips.

Around the time he was two and I was nine I got his mother's story by eavesdropping during one of the agency visits. She had five or six other kids she could barely afford to care for or feed. I also suspect she was one of the ones recovering from drugs. I never heard anyone say those words; it was a feeling I had from her vibration. She reminded me of the drug addicts one of my aunts had a bad habit of dating. Apparently that was my aunt's type. Anyway during the visit Tyrone's mother saw how content he was with my mother so she asked my mother to adopt him.

So when I was ten and he was three my parents legally adopted him. He went from temp to perm as they would say in the administrative assistant world. At first I was not crazy about the idea. I had gotten used to the borrowed siblings being returned. I liked being the youngest permanent stay. But the thought of having someone to always boss around perked me right up.

One of my earlier memories of Tyrone is that same year. My cousin Bettina visits us from Westbury. She sits on our back porch steps while she feeds Tyrone, who is two, a sandwich. A chicken runs into our backyard distracting Bettina. Our next-door neighbor, Mr. Jackson, who has a chicken coop in his backyard, chases his escaped chicken.

Mr. Jackson's chicken coop in the middle of Queens was a constant source of gossip and conversation in my neighborhood. Most of the old women were convinced Mr. Jackson practiced voodoo and that he sacrificed the chickens to cast evil spells. Most of the men thought he was weird. A few neighbors suspected he just really liked fresh chicken for dinner.

So while Bettina watches Mr. Jackson chase his loose chicken she mindlessly stuffs Tyrone's mouth with the sandwich until his cheeks puff out like a chipmunk. The chicken's loud clucking draws the rest of the family and me out to the backyard. It is only then that Bettina notices Tyrone's mouth is too full. Thankfully she has a napkin and he can spit out most of the food before choking. I remember how cute he looked with his cheeks puffed out and the confusion on his face. I always wondered if he was confused by all the food in his mouth, the live chicken chase, or both.

4. Taylor. Sisters.

Taylor arrived when she was three and I was five. She was the color of dark-buckwheat honey, thin, delicate-boned, with big almond-shaped eyes. Taylor stayed the longest—until she was eight and I was ten. She was my main source of sibling rivalry. God bless her. It made me extremely resourceful.

Taylor is the one I played with and envied. In first grade I was expected to bring home my Friday pretzels and candy, rewards for good behavior during the week, and share with Taylor. A task I openly resented since she was not the one being rewarded for good behavior. But I did it because it was expected. Secretly I loved the joy it gave her each week. She especially loved anything cherry-flavored.

Taylor is the one I played house with and went through the Sears catalog with compiling our Christmas lists to Santa each year. Taylor is the one whose bags I happily packed when she threatened to run away because I was mean to her. After all, why should I run away? I was there first. Of course my mother did not see it that way and I had to unpack her bags. I had to put her things away neatly at that, adding insult to injury.

By default Taylor was my little sister. Really there was no foster about it. I never acknowledged that then and only recently as an adult.

My father died when I was ten so that it is when my family stopped providing foster care. My mother felt it was too much for her to do on her own. So we moved to Maryland leaving Taylor to go back to her birth mother, a teenage mother, who was by then an adult and financially stable enough to care for Taylor.

During the time we were in Maryland and Taylor was in New York she and my mother kept in touch through letter-writing and phone calls. During her early twenties Taylor moved to Maryland to be close to us. So Taylor unofficially adopted my family as her own. She is family now without question.

Providing foster care was one of the best things that happened to my family and me. It extended our family and my capacity to love. In addition to my two older sisters, I gained a younger brother and sister. I also learned at an early age that things are never as they seem on the surface. Through my direct experience I realized love is a choice made over and over again. Most importantly, being part of a foster family taught me that love expressed daily in word and action is all there really is to give to another person.

ASSATA

Assata grew up in New York City where she experienced life in two group homes before leaving the system. From her experience in the system, she says she's developed the: "perseverance, determination, and the ability to face life head-on, no matter what the issue is." Through her essay "Riding the E-Train to Here," she describes her journey from foster care to becoming a successful career woman and mother of a three-year-old daughter. She believes that foster children are not stunted people who are to be pitied, and encourages all children currently in the system to realize that "this experience does not define you. If you can make it in this system, the world is yours!!!"

RIDING THE E-TRAIN TO HERE

By Assata

For all intents and purposes my life story reads like a fairy tale. A young girl goes from sleeping on New York City trains to the hallowed halls of the University of Chicago. The journey is far less romantic than it sounds, but it is beautiful nonetheless. The experience of homelessness and foster care reverberates through my life. Its impact is glimpsed in my drive to succeed, an amazing ability to persevere as all around me crumbles and a propensity for guerilla warfare tactics (fight and run) in the face of major changes, loss and emotional challenges. My struggle to create stability in my life and emotional boundaries of loving deeply but showing little are direct by-products of my childhood and foster care experience.

The only child of a short dalliance between my mother and father, I spent my formative years in Barbados being raised by family members. I received love and support from my maternal aunts and paternal grandmother, father, and stepmother. I was raised Caribbean style. This meant beating with tamarind rods, days of going to the beach and playing on the pasture, visiting family and pitching marbles outside of my great-aunt's house. Despite the molestation by a maternal great-uncle and a loneliness that permeated my soul, I was okay.

When I was three years old, my mother immigrated to the United States to achieve the "American dream." I would not physically see her again until I was nine years old on a hot summer night at JFK Airport. I was extremely excited and nervous about meeting my mother. For many years I'd experienced my mother through phone calls, pictures, letters, and the barrels full of supplies she shipped to Barbados for my cousin and me.

Finally, I would get to see, touch, and hold a living breathing woman. I was unprepared for the woman I saw. She did not resemble the glamorous woman I expected from the pictures of her time in Las Vegas. Gone were the impeccable makeup, long Jheri-curled hair and pretty clothes. Instead, I was greeted by a woman in a jacket with tight jeans, dirty sneakers and short permed hair that was brushed back. There was no makeup, nothing distinctive. I was in shock—I alternated between joy at seeing my mother after all these years, and disappointment for she did not resemble the woman I envisioned. I am sure that the awkward, chubby nine-year-old that deplaned that day was not what she had expected. I thought I looked great. After all, my stepmother had bought us, my brothers and me, new outfits for the trip to "away." I wore pedal-pushers with socks and sneakers. My hair was braided nicely with barrettes. I am sure I appeared "country" to the New York eyes of my mother.

This visit to New York was not the dream I thought it would be. New York, with its graffitied trains and abandoned buildings, did not resemble the city I saw in movies and television shows. Americans, most of all Black Americans, did not speak the way Robert Urich did in *Vegas* (my heartthrob at the time) or the people on *Sesame Street*. My mother's existence was not the glamorous life I envisioned based on her stories and American television shows. My mother did not live in a huge apartment and was not well-off. She and her husband, at that time, fought like cats and dogs. That summer was emotionally tumultuous for a nine-year-old. Dreams were dashed; anger and abandonment reared its head. There was a deep dark pit that my mother's presence did little to fill.

Even during this brief visit I remember writing of wanting to run away. My mother found my notes and was hurt. She tried talking to me; I did not have the words to explain how I felt nor the courage to share what I could explain. My nine-year-old mind was trying to sort out things, I was unprepared to understand. Despite the thrill of being "away" and the bragging rights I would have at school, I was still unhappy. A year later at the age of ten, I tucked away these feelings and rejoiced at the prospect of living with my mother, the idolized stranger who lived "away." The opportunity was too good to be true. The move was a bittersweet affair that would forever change my life. My mother and I were unprepared for the experience.

Our romanticized view of each other was so far from reality, that we rarely speak to this day. When we do communicate, it is with the cordiality of people who are linked by a shared experience in the old neighborhood, but have little else in common. Our inability to weather abandonment issues and unrealistic expectations of each other led to my stay in the foster care system. Life with my mother was never easy. The honeymoon was soon over, if it ever began at all.

From the beginning of my new life in New York, I felt as if I was an embarrassment to my mother. This was further exacerbated by the changes that had occurred in my mother's life during the year after my visit. Specifically, my mother had met a new man and was pregnant. The time I envisioned us spending together did not happen. She was in love, preparing for motherhood and creating her dream family. I felt like an interloper in the picture; the family member recruited from home to play the maid.

It did not help that my ten-year-old "new immigrant" Barbadian ways irritated my mother. She made it clear that New York was not a place where people help each other. One must do everything for yourself and in this case—her. I was put on a diet of smaller portions: one protein, one starch and a lot of vegetables because I was too fat. In my mother's eyes anything bigger than Nicole Richie and the Olsen twins was considered fat. At dinner if I committed the ultimate sin of holding the fork between my second and third digits, I would lose my eating privileges for the night, being sent to bed early. Soon the beatings began. The infractions ranged from I did not move fast enough and I was dirty to I had a "don't-careish" look on my face. I remember getting my finger dislocated during a beating with a lamp. This injury would be my first introduction to the concept of the foster care system.

I was in sixth grade at the neighborhood elementary school when the incident occurred. My hand was so swollen that my teacher noticed it during the course of the day and sent me to the principal's office immediately. The principal met with me to inquire about the injury. She asked questions that ranged from how often I was beaten to if the beatings left marks to if I was scared of my mother. I became afraid when she spoke of calling the police or having someone remove me from my home. I knew my mother would never forgive me if that happened. More importantly, as a new immigrant, I was petrified. Although I had my green card, I knew no one outside of family members. I was already being teased about my accent and academic ability; what would life be like living with American strangers? I did not want to find out. I lied; simply, beautifully and calmly. I told my principal that it was a freak accident, that I was not beaten frequently.

She accepted the lies as easily as I told them. It made her job easier. I believe she used the words "silver lining on a dark cloud" to commend my academic success and acceptance to a magnet junior high school in the midst of this trouble. Nonetheless, they could not keep me in school with such an obvious and serious injury. My mother was called and we went to the hospital room where my finger was set and I received a lollipop and kudos for my bravery. This was not the end of my emotional and physical abuse. It continued and would worsen over the years. I always wondered if my experience would have been different, if I'd told the truth.

The beatings continued. I received them for not mopping the floor properly. I would be woken up by cold water being thrown on my face for whatever wrongs, imagined or actual, I'd committed. As the beatings and verbal abuse increased, so did my stealing. I would take dimes, quarters and dollars to buy candy and sunflower seeds. As a result I would have my hand held over the lit stove with a promise to burn it if I did not stop stealing.

At home I did nothing right. At school I excelled, even if I did not do my homework—my grades were impressive. The nights of my mother packing my clothes in black garbage bags as she described the horrors of living in a group home occurred at least once a month. Our next-door neighbor, Mama Sunshine, would often find me sleeping on the shared landing and beg my mother to let me back into the house.

Months of this soon became too difficult for me to endure. In seventh grade I ran away to a family friend's house. "Godmother," as she was called, knew my family for many years. Although she had four daughters of her own who lived with her, Godmother's home was a haven for everyone else's children. She took in the abandoned and abused. Godmother's home was also a conduit to life in New York. Many of her friends and family from Barbados sent their children to live with her so that they could have a chance to achieve the "American dream." Living at Godmother's house was a haven. I got to see another side of life that I had not experienced. I had fun with the other girls who lived there. Some were older, others my age-mates, yet, I missed the solitude I could have at my mother's house and going to the museums in the city, among other activities. This paradise did not last long and soon I returned to my mother's house. This moving around would set the tone for my teenage years. I spent much of these years moving around between family members until I became homeless.

There was no horrible story to my homelessness. One evening after being told to "get out," I packed some clothes and left. I came home late that day and I was supposed to do the laundry. I did not do it and knew my mother would be upset. She came home, beat me and told me to get out. Tired of being beaten and ridiculed, I did. I did not know where I was going; I only knew that I could not take it any longer. It was then that I started riding the trains. My plan was to sleep on the trains from evening to morning and take a shower/wash-up at school. I kept my clothes in a locker at school until some of them were thrown out during the change in the semester.

My homelessness was particularly disappointing as it began a week or two before my sixteenth birthday. My mother had already crafted the perfect American "Sweet Sixteen" party and story. I envisioned a party where all of my friends would come to chill and listen to music. My mother would finally be able to meet the people who kept me sane in the midst of all the madness. She dreamed of a coming-out party with frills and bows. Neither of those dreams occurred for me. Instead, the night I turned sixteen I was sitting in a diner listening to three people sing "whiffy woman" to the refrains of "Pretty Woman" and give me a bottle of cologne. Maybe they did not know that I had nowhere to go. That the reason I smelled was because my home was the "A-train." No one knew that I rode the trains; that I stopped sleeping on the "A-Train" at night because I once woke up to a find a crackhead trying to steal my bag of clothes. I fought and fought until I had to give a few shirts away so I could be left alone. No one knew that I moved to the L-train because it had the best heat but soon left that train because I could not get a full night's sleep. The L-train was unsafe, I feared for my life when it neared Canarsie. So, I moved to the D-train, riding from Fifty-Ninth Street in Manhattan to Stillwell Avenue in Coney Island. When that ride became too short for me to get a good night's sleep because I feared riding all the way to the Bronx, I moved to the E-train. The E-train became my haven. I could ride from the World Trade Center to Queens in virtual safety with good heat. If I was not sleeping in the pool hall I frequented, an aunt's house or a stranger's place, the E-train was where I could be found.

The first half of my sixteenth year passed in a haze. During that year, I slept on New York City trains and went clubbing in New York hotspots like Mars, The Bank and Red Zone, while trying to figure out where I could take a bath and get some sleep. It was during this year that I ended up at the Covenant House Girls Group Home on Forty-Seventh Street in Hell's Kitchen. Somehow, God and my ancestors kept me alive in the midst of those six months. That short time felt like ten years in my life. I do not have the space to recount all of the details of that time, however, here are a few examples of some of my experiences during that time.

There was an older man I met in the pool hall where I hung out. He was always circumspect and respectful and even bought me food sometimes. He was aware of my situation and frequently talked to me about going home. I thought he was cool, so when he offered me a place to stay for the evening, I thought it would be okay to accept. He lived in a great loft in Brooklyn with other artists. He allowed me to take a bath, eat and relax. I fell asleep to the sound of jazz in a warm bed with covers, however, like others before him, he tried to have sex with me. I fought back and luckily my struggles and his conscience stopped him from doing more. He came to his senses, stopped and apologized profusely; however, the damage was done. Needless to say, I did not sleep that night and had few words for him after that episode. Then there was the time I convinced a Spanish guy that we'd actually had sex even as he came on his sheets. He thought he was in love, I was hoping he did not find out he'd been duped. I pressed on, feeling isolated and abandoned in the midst of those different experiences. That was until I met Jerry, my guardian angel.

Jerry was a club kid who dealt cocaine to make money. He was in the midst of a personal crisis—he was unsure of his sexuality. He was attracted to me and that's how we met. Jerry never tried anything with me; he was also a transient moving between his brother and friends. He introduced me to even more of the club life. Jerry knew DJ Dimitry and would take me along with him to meet all of the club kids at McDonald's on Broadway in the Village to get the word for the night; a word that would get us into clubs for free. I call Jerry my guardian angel because he was the one who took me to Covenant House. Maybe he was trying to get me off his hands— I don't know. I am clear that whatever his reason, he saved my life that night. It was the middle of winter, it was cold and we were being kicked out of the pool hall.

So, Jerry, tired of fighting for a place to stay, suggested we go to Covenant House. I trusted him, so I went. We arrived at Covenant House around two a.m. It was us and a few other young people. We were interviewed separately and then sent to gender-based dorms to sleep. In the morning when I woke up, I knew Jerry would be gone. I spoke with him briefly that day and never heard from him again. He was twenty-seven, so I am not sure how he conned his way into the program for the night, but he was one of many who found a way. By the second day, I was moved from sleeping on a cot in a large living room at the under-twenty-one site, to the Girl's Group Home on Forty-Seventh Street. This was a godsend— I was finally able to sleep without worrying about being raped, groped or losing the little clothes I had left. More importantly, I had a stable place to stay for at least a month.

My experience at this group home shattered many of the myths and fears I had about living in a group home. Fueled by my mother's stories and movies of young women in detention centers, I was prepared to fight for my life. Instead, I found other young women, like myself, who were fighting for themselves in the midst of being homeless and abused. We hid our fear behind bravado and complaining about our curfew. We shared stories of life, parties, and boys before the group home. We tried getting high by putting toothpaste on Newport cigarettes, and hung out with teenage boys and older guys who tried to prey on us because we lived in a group home. As I would soon learn, boys in the neighborhood always knew where the girl's group homes were located and enjoyed the revolving door of "new meat" that the group-home process provided. After hanging out a few times, I stopped when I discovered that the price was for me to "put out."

Typically girls were placed in the Forty-Seventh Street group home for thirty days. I had the blessing of being there for three months. The staff at the Forty-Seventh Street home fought for me to be placed in a good group home. They waited until a placement became available in a group home they liked, sent me there for a day to see if it was a match, and were excited that I gave it an okay. So three months after my arrival, I took the famed foster kid walk. My clothes were packed in that clear plastic bag that every foster child knows so well. It holds our clothes, pictures, arts & crafts—small remnants of our lives, the places we've been, and the people we've encountered. I rode the E-train to the G-train, alone with my possessions and my thoughts. It was a familiar feeling considering the last six months of my life; except this time I had a destination.

Unsure of what I would find in this group home, I imagined the worst. Even though I'd already visited, my experience had taught me that things are rarely as they appear. Although I trusted the staff at Covenant House, adults did not have a good track record with me. What I found there was completely unexpected.

The Salvation Army group home was one of the few places where I was able to experience the totality of my being. All of the expectations placed on my shoulders faded into dust. The young women I met there taught me more about myself than I can share.

It was here where I was able to meet Filomena, who introduced me to Black Sabbath, the Lower East Side punk life, and loved Metallica as much as I did. A Caribbean child, Fil was always mysterious. To this day I have never figured out why she was placed in foster care, yet we bonded and still speak occasionally. Desiree and Trina fostered the Brooklyn Hip-Hop chick in me. Desiree was my roommate and a young girl who'd spent most of her life in foster care. She was extremely funny but quick to anger. Outside of the group-home trips and hanging out in the house, we did not spend a lot of time together. Actually, Desiree and I were known to have huge fights and then fifteen minutes later crack jokes with each other.

Patty was one of the two white girls in the group home. She'd spent much of her adolescence in the group home and was biding her time until she could be on her own. Patty and I went to a Sting concert when she won tickets on the radio. We often spoke about our dreams of escaping the group home. When we both got jobs, we would laugh over our ordeal of having to "slurp water." Essentially, "slurping water" was the poor man's lunch; one drank water from the water fountain at work when you started a new job and could not afford to buy lunch.

There was Nef—overweight with buck teeth and glasses; she wore an amour of funk like a shield. Nef's aversion to bathing, doing laundry, and being clean made her the pariah of the group. Since we shared a room there was many arguments and Lysol sprayings. However, Nefertiti could also be the sweetest person, and in some instances, became the group-home bank when we ran out of our allowance and needed extra cash.

Finally, there was Ana Celia Nieves. Ana was a slight Puerto-Rican young woman who was twenty but looked fourteen. We were both Libras who refused to be pigeon-holed. Many times, we did not need to communicate because we knew each other so well. Ana and I shared many exciting times together. We would just as soon drink 40's of Olde English with the thugs on the block as trip on mescaline and go to white-boy frat parties at NYU.

We had loads of fun in the group home. We actually sneaked the rapper Tragedy, "The Intelligent Hoodlum," and his dancer into our rooms one night. Since the group home was actually a combined apartment in Lefrak City apartments, we were able to have night visitors climb onto the supermarket and enter our windows to hang out. The overnight child care worker was an elderly woman who quickly fell asleep after smoking her Kool cigarettes (which we would steal) and watching TV. It meant that we could stay up past our curfew and do things we were not supposed to do. In the morning we were always greeted by her greasy, oily grits for breakfast. To this day, I do not eat grits.

Ancha was our den mother; she kept the entire house together. Ancha was an older Black American with Southern roots. We responded to her as a mother figure. Ancha meted out wisdom, discipline, humor and our weekly and shopping allowances like a mother. She bore the brunt of our anger, tears, and petty arguments as any mother would. She gave sage wisdom as our grandmothers did. Hugs, a tongue lashing and the honor of sitting in her office talking were the rewards we all sought.

I spent much of my time in the group home on restriction. This would usually occur because I broke curfew and "AWOL'd" regularly, more like clockwork. One could be sure that as soon as I got off restriction for one offense, I would stay out all night or receive permission to go home for weekend visits, but never arrived there. Like clockwork, my mother would call the group home to see where I was, which meant that as soon as I returned to the group home, I was placed on a one- or two-week restriction. The punishment was always worth the crime.

I cannot say that my time in the group home was horrible. I do not have the horror stories that many people have of their time in foster care. It was in the Salvation Army group home where I found the stability I needed to return to school. It allowed me a safe space to return to some semblance of a normal life—to routine. It was in the midst of this experience that I was able to come to terms with myself—an African-Caribbean girl who liked heavy metal and drinking 40's of Olde E. I could hang out with white boys in the village; go clubbing and still chill with the thugs in Lefrak (Lef-Crack) City. The Salvation Army took us on trips to Washington, D.C. and Virginia. We took trips with the other Salvation Army group homes to dude ranches and sat through Life Skill classes together. For the young women in the home, we all struggled with loving and finding ourselves in the midst of rejection, abandonment and the stigma of being in the foster care system.

However, the excitement and fun of being in the group home was tempered by the trials of twelve young women living together. My emotional shell was hardened at the hands of their betrayals. I learned that when you live with women, vindictiveness is innate. One must develop guerilla warfare tactics in order to survive and keep your battered dignity intact. In the group home we lived together, fought, and comforted each other. We learned about life at its essence. It was during this time that I made the choice to become a social worker, to fight for the marginalized youth, the keys to our future, who are routinely demonized.

After a year and a half in "the system," I returned to my mother's house. Even though I enjoyed most of the time in the group home, I also knew that foster care was not for me. Maybe it was the arrogance of my Barbadian upbringing and mother's training, but I knew that this place was not where I should try to spend my teenage years. Within six months of returning to my mother's house, I was living with a man I hardly knew—entering adulthood in a way I did not plan. I completed high school by attending night school but I was still able to receive my diploma from a prestigious New York City High School. I worked for a year and matriculated at Adelphi University in the fall of 1993.

In 1998, I graced the hallowed halls of the University of Chicago and graduated two years later with my degree. My story continues. I still struggle with the effects of physical and sexual abuse and the fear of being unable to protect my child from these ills. But I do it with the strength of my experience; knowing that journey I took—knowing it will always be right. Throughout the years, my experience on the streets of New York and in the foster care system has been my burden and shame. It has at times been my badge of honor and a chip on my shoulder. Now, I have made peace with it. The experience of reviewing and sharing that time of my life has been liberating and challenging; there is so much I have omitted, so much left to say. The journey is not complete. I am still learning to be a better person and mother. I am working on moving forward and forging a new path that is not steeped in the past. It is a challenge—I press on.

ARNITA WHITE

Arnita White's essay, "My Life: the Child of a Foster Mom," tells the story of "Keith," a young boy taken in by her mother and ultimately given back to his biological family. Through her exposure to foster care, Arnita says that she learned what the word "family" really means, and that you don't have to be born into a family to truly be a part of it. The mother of three children of her own, Arnita feels the foster care system can often move children around too much, making it hard for them to put down roots and feel secure in one home. Though she still feels the pain of her brother "Keith" no longer being in her life, she says that she has learned to accept this loss: "I have made the decision to be happy. I know this is a choice and I know that no one else can make me happy...It has taken me years to get to this point but it feels great. I am happy."

MY LIFE:
THE CHILD OF A FOSTER MOM

By Arnita White

My mom was a foster mother for as far back as I can remember. She chose to be a single mother because she did not want to marry. I was the youngest of her five children, yet we were all affected in some way by these strangers that had to live with us and share our space—even if it was for a little while. At a very young age, I learned becoming emotionally attached just spelled trouble.

Mom took in all ages of children with problems, including babies. The baby that made the biggest impact on all of our lives was brought to us by a caseworker when he was only three days old. We named him "Keith," but his real name was Tyson. His mother was an alcoholic and all of her seven children had been placed in foster care, but we only got Keith. He was raised as our very own little brother and the funny thing about it was he looked like my favorite uncle so he fit right in. Everybody believed he was ours and we would not let them think anything different. Keith was a smart and loving little boy. We all protected him and would do anything in the world for him.

My mother was the glue that kept the family together so we always had a house full of people, family and friends. Our house was the meeting place. Keith was right there with us through it all. We definitely spoiled him rotten.

When Keith turned five years old, my mother decided she should adopt him. In those days it was very hard for a single mother to adopt, so mom notified Social Services and Child Services of her intentions and was told to get married. Knowing that getting married was the only way to get Keith, she decided to do so in order to adopt him. She never should have done that.

Keith's mother was notified about mom's plans and was told that she could get her child back if she still wanted him. The mother was not given visitation to get to know her son before taking him home, even though she had not seen her son since he was three days old, if ever. His mother lived in the next community over from ours, so actually she walked to our home that day to take him away from us. When she arrived at the gate of our front yard, we could hear our dog, King, barking madly. King clearly didn't like Keith's mother, and would not let her into the yard. We came out of the house to see what the problem was, and there she stood, at the gate. She said that she was Tyson's mother, and was there to take him home. We all looked at each other wondering who is this Tyson she was talking about and how could she be taking him home. Then we remembered Keith is Tyson, but she didn't need to take him anywhere, he was already home.

This woman looked crazy and drunk to us. My mother looked at us, then told us there was nothing we could do except let him go. Keith (well, Tyson) began screaming and crying, trying to run back inside which made all of us start crying, even my mother. Mom picked Tyson up and carried him to her. We stood there sobbing, not believing what was happening. His mother did not hold him and carry him like my mom did. She just stood him on the ground and told him to shut up, he was going with her. We stood on the porch and watched Keith and his mother until we could see them no more. Mom walked toward us, made us all turn around and walk inside the house. We cried for days. Soon it would be Christmas, so to cheer us up, Mom decided we should all go out shopping to get gifts for Keith.

Mom knew where Keith lived, so on Christmas morning she took us over to his house. We couldn't wait to see him again. We got there, knocked on the door and waited and waited. We knocked some more, then a voice yelled at us to go away. His mother knew who we were and yelled again that if we didn't leave she was going to beat Tyson. He heard our voices through the door and started crying for us. Mama told us to come on and leave. We cried all the way home. Mama sat us down that day and told us the best thing we could do for Keith was to leave him alone and to forget about him, or his mother would hurt him.

I later discovered that his brothers went to my school, so I made sure I found out who they were so I could meet them. I could tell from our first meeting that one of them liked me. I tried to be his girlfriend so that I could go over to his house to see Keith. My brother met Keith's brothers, too, and he ended up being friends with both brothers. Soon after, we started going over their way to play with them, hoping Keith would come out, too. We asked the brothers about him and found out that the mother really was beating him because he kept crying for us and would not answer to Tyson. His mother wouldn't let him out of the house until many years later. We eventually lost touch with the brothers because their family moved to keep Keith away from us.

My mother decided she did not want to be a foster mother to any more children after losing Keith, but a social worker came to the house and begged her to take one more baby. When Mama agreed, she was given a little mixed baby girl to take care of. This baby was only three days old when the case worker brought her to our house. Her mother couldn't take her home because, being white, her family would not accept a baby fathered by a black man. The baby did not have a name so my mother asked me if I wanted to name her. I was so excited. I named her Shantee but I could not spell it so she was called Shani. The case worker found Shani a home and she left us about three months later. She was one of the cutest babies I had ever seen. Mom never accepted any more children.

I became an advocate for children in my school that were picked on or too scared to stand up for themselves. I was not a bully, but I fought for the underdog or walked them to class to make sure nothing happened to these weak or scared children. I gave lessons on protecting themselves. I knew my little brother would need someone to stand up for him, and because I could be there for him, I stood up for others in his situation. I also learned to be more understanding because for years I tried to understand Keith's mother treating him so badly.

Twenty years later, I was working at a grocery store and a young man came to my register. For no apparent reason, when I saw this young man I started shaking and crying. I couldn't believe it. It was Keith! I didn't know if anyone had ever told him about being with us so I looked at him and said, "You look so familiar."

He said, "You look familiar to me, too." I told him I remembered him as a little boy. He didn't say another word. He simply began to cry and walked out of the store. I wanted to grab him and hug and kiss him. My little brother stood right in front of me and I couldn't even say anything because I was afraid I would hurt him even more. I couldn't work any more that day. That was one of the happiest and saddest days of my life. I went to Mom's house that evening because the family was getting together for the first time in a long time. I told them all about seeing Keith and they were upset with me for not telling him who I was. I looked for Keith every day that I worked at that grocery store. He never showed up again. I was going to tell him who I was the next time I saw him, how much I missed and loved him.

Having my little brother, Keith, in my life, then suddenly be taken away has affected me every day. I am still looking for him. I even told my children about Keith. I would love to be able to meet him and have him as a part of my family again.

No one, especially a child, should have to go through losing someone they love and know that he/she is still alive. After growing up and not being able to forget this very painful and emotional experience, I believe foster care should allow a child to become permanently adopted after so many years in the foster home—for the sake of all involved. Maybe the foster parent needs the money provided for taking care of this foster child, but the foster home should eventually become a permanent home for the child. The foster child should not have to worry about someone coming to take them away from the only home they know. A foster system that allows a total stranger, albeit a parent, to take a child away from the only home he/she knows without setting up meetings to introduce the child and parent is neglectful of that child. The child needs to know what is happening before he is taken away from the only home he has known.

PATT FREEMAN-MIHAILOFF

Patt Freeman-Mihailoff's story is rare in foster care. Entering her mother's home at age nine, she stayed until the age of 28 when she married. Her parents were once named "Foster Parents of the Year" for two consecutive years by the New York City Child Care Association. In her parents' home, she says she faced no physical or mental abuse, and was "treated like their own daughter." Through her foster mother's help at the age of twelve, she was able to find her biological brother who lived in another foster home not far from where she lived. Now a well-adjusted and thriving adult, she credits her success in life to her foster mother. She says, "I am the person I am today... because of the prayers a wonderful woman invoked by a higher power who helped her every step of the way, to lead me into teen, young womanhood, and now in the middle years of my life. I have purpose, joy, and love, and it was all because of her."

TRIAL BASIS

By Pat Freeman-Mihailoff

There are words a child should never hear her father say like: "I don't want her," or have her mother confirm it with: "I don't want her, either." It's funny how I didn't remember those words until much later in life, but there they were. When you're little, size and distance are relative. Everything else seems so big. From the house you live in, to the short train ride that feels long and takes you to a new life.

At the age of six I'd seen things a child should never see, and heard things a child should never hear. Abuse doesn't always come in the physical form, but can attach itself to you in a memory that will never allow you to forget how you *might* have turned out.

I remember both my birth parents, but I never remembered us living together as a family. I was usually with one or the other at different times, even though they often lived within shouting distance of each other.

Back then, Negroes, as we were called, were relegated to a long line of dilapidated row houses extending from one corner of the beach streets that ran up to the boardwalk. I surmise now that if they'd known how much that property would eventually be worth, they would have maintained custody of it. But what they hadn't let slip through their hands, they gave away, like I was given away.

When I was six and a half, my mother lived with her current boyfriend across the street from my father and his mysterious paramour, an enigmatic woman I had to call "Ms. Catherine." She was a small, quiet, dark-skinned woman who never spoke to me and in fact, the only sounds I ever heard from her were moans invoked by my father when they made love.

One day, my mom and her friend were having a knock-down, drag-out fight, which was common with them. I didn't like the yelling so I started making my way up toward the boardwalk. My mother always told me never to walk up near the boardwalk, and later in life I understood why. Too many things were going on under there, from drugs to the most decadent sex acts. Little did I know that what would happen to me that day would have nothing to do with the things going on underneath the boardwalk, but on top of it, and at the hands of my own mother.

A moment after arriving at the end of the boardwalk, I heard my mother call me and I ran back and took my place on the creaky wooden steps as though I'd done nothing wrong. After a few minutes I felt a burning sensation on my backside and my legs, and because I had been leaning back, soon my arms were also in stinging pain. I began to scratch and rub, and when I looked, there was blood on my fingers and my shorts were tattered as though something had eaten through them. I began to scream as the burning got worse. The next thing I remember was my father taking me to Queens General Hospital where I was immersed in a cold substance as I screamed for dear life.

Later on I learned that when my mother and her friend were arguing, she threatened to pour potash (lye) on his face, but he twisted her arm and it spilled onto the steps. Because it was crystalline clear, I didn't see it before sitting down. When I returned from the hospital, my father brought me home. I slept on a bare mattress he put on the kitchen floor and in pajamas that he had fashioned out of two of his long-sleeved white shirts. I eventually healed from my wounds, but it wouldn't be long before I would be hurt again due to the lack of supervision in my parents' homes.

About a year or so later I bumped my head while spinning around a rusted "no parking" sign, even after a passerby told me I should stop. Back into the hospital I went, only this time, they had to strap me down as the doctors picked out rusted particles of metal from an open wound above my left eye, leaving a scar that I carry to this day. It wouldn't be long before my parents would decide that caring for me was more than they were prepared to do.

One day I was playing in the front room when my father called out to me. I ran in, and there was my mother and Miss M., my father's girlfriend at the time, sitting at her small square kitchen table. I climbed onto his lap as I often did when he wasn't playing cards or drinking. I don't recall what I was playing with on the table, but I do remember scraps of conversation as my father spoke, and the last words from my mother which were: "Well, I don't want her, either."

It didn't faze me then, because I was sure they were not talking about me. But they were, and the next thing I knew I was living with my great-aunt Minnie, or Aunt Min as I called her. She was a tall, tree-bark-brown-hued, rail-thin woman with blue hair. Back then, women with gray hair always put a blue rinse in it for some strange reason I didn't understand, but I loved the way she'd pull it up into the biggest French twist I'd ever seen.

She lived in a small three-room apartment on the top floor of a two-story building situated on a main street of a deteriorating Polish-Italian neighborhood. The remaining impoverished Poles didn't like that Negroes were moving in, especially since Aunt Min got what they thought of as a choice apartment in the front, instead of the ramshackle house with part of the roof missing in the back.

There was something regal about the way Aunt Min carried herself, and everyone seemed to have a heavy respect for her. She had an eclectic group of friends and relatives that ranged from her white male friend—a real no-no at that time—who owned a junk store a few blocks away, to her best friend Oleta who dipped snuff and spat the brown dripping mess into empty Coca-Cola bottles. Then there was her brother, Uncle Johnny, a "rummy" as she called him, who only came around sporadically with his toothless mouth full of drink and jokes.

Aunt Minnie didn't have much, but whatever she had, she shared with me. I became her child, and she made sure I ate right, went to school, and behaved with the threat of whippings she never gave me. She read the Bible but I don't recall her ever going to church. I went to Our Lady of Sorrows Roman Catholic Church two blocks away where a handsome young priest named Father Joseph caught me and another girl climbing up on the full-sized male plaster saint to practice our kissing techniques.

Aunt Min liked what she called her "little nip every now and then," and would take me with her to the corner bar owned by an Italian couple that kept me supplied with large glasses of ginger ale with three cherries. They also made sure I had plenty of bananas because they knew I loved them so much, and there was a pinball machine that the owner fiddled with so that I could play without putting in any money. I was never allowed in the actual bar area, but they let me play in the empty back room where I later learned, late-night high-stakes poker games took place. I enjoyed living with Aunt Min, and I hoped to stay there forever, but in my world, forever was never guaranteed.

One day I came home from school and a young pinch-nosed white woman was seated in the front room. I entered the room and leaned against Aunt Min who hugged me to her, but didn't look at me as she spoke to the woman. "...And she can't spend one single day in a shelter," was all I heard.

Time and distance can confuse a child, It seemed like months later, when it was in fact only a week or two, when Aunt Min told me that she wasn't able to care for me anymore and I was going to visit a new family. Aunt Min was sick, but I'd had no idea. I only remember that her happy face was drawn, her expression had grown solemn, and her smile was sad whenever she looked at me. I didn't understand and I remember crying, but not much more. A little while after that, the same state case worker showed up and told me she was taking me to meet the new family. Back then, you didn't meet anybody wearing pants or shorts, and Aunt Min dressed me in the nicest frock I owned, with new shoes and socks to impress my potential new family.

The train ride seemed to take forever, and because I had never been out of my area, I leaned against the window, peering at the houses and trains that whizzed by us. Little did I know then that I was on the Long Island Rail Road, and we were only going a few stops. A cab ride later and we were at a huge house situated across the street from a school, with a long tree-lined island separating the two. I had been told that the lady I was going to see already had two foster boys, but I had no idea what that meant.

"This is only a visit. If she likes you, it will be on a trial basis," the case worker said.

"Why?" I asked, but she didn't answer and I later learned that I was a bit old for people to foster because usually they wanted babies or kids no older than three. The woman of the house appeared tall to me, but in reality she was not more than five feet two inches or so. She had black hair, a round friendly face, and the prettiest smile I ever saw. She introduced herself and told me that "the boys," who were both younger than me, were playing downstairs in the family room. "Wow!" I thought, this house was bigger than any I had ever been in.

She made lunch and I met her husband who was so tall I had to lean back to look up at him. The case worker watched us for a bit, then went off with the couple to talk while I played with the two little boys. When we got back to Aunt Min's, she and the case worker talked in hushed tones, and again I was excluded. That night Aunt Min cuddled me close and told me the most devastating news.

"I'm not able to take care of you anymore, but I think we might have found a good home for you."

"With that lady I saw today?"

"Yes, but it's only on a trial basis, so you have to be a good girl." Soon after, I visited the nice lady's house again. When I returned this time, Aunt Min told me she was going to be my new mother. There must have been some kind of instinct because at that time the two women had never met.

Finally the case worker came and took me and a single suitcase and brought me back to the place I was to call home. When I walked into the house that day I don't know what happened, except that it was as though God was somewhere in that room and said: "This child needs a mother, and this mother needs a daughter."

Before she left, the case worker again told me it was only on a trial basis, but when that nice lady smiled at me and held out her arms, I said one word: "Mom," and I've been saying it for over forty years. I later learned that Aunt Min was terminally ill and that was why she couldn't keep me. She didn't want to send me back to my parents because number one, they didn't want me, and second, she knew the environment was unsuitable. My foster mother and Aunt Min got to meet before she died and I could tell by the look on her face that she knew she had made the right decision.

The trial basis turned into a lifetime of love and friendship with me giving my mom as much aggravation, pain, scary moments, and joy as any real daughter can give a mother. Because of her, I am what I am today, and the eight-year-old little girl I once was grew into a woman of spirit, grace, and integrity.

I saw my birth mother only once after that. It was at her funeral when I was nineteen. The tears that welled in my eyes were not because of her, but because she never cared to see what I had become. As my unfamiliar relatives crowded around me and asked me to stay, I politely declined and went home to the only mother I wanted to know, and who remains the very best friend I'll ever have.

ROSE GARLAND

Rose Garland is a survivor of eleven foster homes before being adopted at the age of thirteen with her brother Jerry. An accomplished woman, she holds a master's degree, and has supported her brother in his pursuits in life, as well as nurturing his passion for art. In spite of the many obstacles she has faced, she says, "I am more than what I came from. I have made it. My brother has made it. Our lives have never been extraordinarily easy, but we have persevered...we certainly don't expect other people to take care of us. We don't make excuses." For kids in the system, she offers these words: "First, I love you. I know what you're going through. Keep dreaming your dreams even though you feel powerless. When the sadness overwhelms you, pray—make friends with God. Speak up! Your voice is important, and it MATTERS." Rose has found her voice through writing and her work as an advocate for children. In this capacity, she asks that anyone in the system currently in need of emotional support or advice, feel free to contact her at: rosegarland1@hotmail.com.

ALL ELSE ASIDE: JERRY AND ME

By Rose Garland

All else aside, our parents were very attractive. Our birth father looked like Elvis, and apparently this was a good thing. Our mother looked like Grace Kelly, and was as intelligent as any foreign diplomat. Mental illness, even paranoid schizophrenia, doesn't keep someone from being very smart, though it can be a hindrance to good parenting. There were originally three of us kids, and we were all taken away from our birth parents really early on.

I like to imagine my brother and me when we were first put in foster care. I was three, and had long, fine blonde hair. My brother was only a month old, and my birth sister had already been adopted by that time. From the beginning, my brother had a hard time. Taken away from our mother at only one month old, we went to several foster homes in a row. He didn't get the stability, love, and care that they say is instrumental to a child between the ages of zero to three. My brother and I have had very similar upbringings, but throughout all of it, he still had it so much harder than I did. Some people might say it's because he's a boy, or because of his learning or behavioral problems, but whatever the true reason is, it's a shame, because like all of us foster kids, my brother deserved better.

My brother and I both experienced every form of abuse there is a label for. In our most abusive home, where I was from the ages of four to nine, and my brother, being three years younger, from one to six, I remember the foster mother getting angry at him and getting ready to punish him—either by locking him in a room, starving him, beating him with something until it broke, or sexually abusing him. And I would do something to get her attention off him. My amazing brother, even at such a young age, learned my trick, and would do something guaranteed to make her even madder, so she would take out her anger on him instead of me. As young as we were, my brother and I stood together. We have always shown each other extreme loyalty, and still, even in our thirties, are the most important people in each other's lives.

I have to admit, I was the "good girl," and the perfect opposite to Jerry—at least on the outside. He always had the hot temper, and I smoothed things out. Like usual in our early relationship years, I took it as my responsibility to teach him everything I knew. Jerry and I always joke about an incident that happened when we were younger, although the consequences of it were not really funny at all. I was twelve, and Jerry was nine. I had been placed for a short-lived "reunification" with my birth mother, and Jerry was able to come for weekend visits twice a month.

One day, Jerry and I were in the back alley of our house in downtown Detroit, and I was teaching him how to light a fire with a shrub and garbage we'd collected from the alley. I assured him I already had done it a bunch of times and it was totally safe. I got the gasoline can out of the garage, took our mother's matches, and proceeded to start a small fire behind the garage in our alley. Suddenly, I saw our social worker running to the back yard as fast as possible—immediately I threw the matches as far from me as possible, and handed the gas can to Jerry, which of course, he got blamed for. I can't even talk about how guilty I feel for that now, but I try to remind myself I was just a kid!

Knowing the foster care system a lot better today than I did then, I am positive that experience was probably written up in his record, and made it even harder to place him than it was before. However, the fact that Jerry and I joke about things like this shows that our relationship has only been enhanced by the things we have endured together.

Jerry and I lived together for the first five years of foster care, and were separated for the next five years. I moved ten times in ten years, and he moved much more often than I did. Jerry says he doesn't have any memories whatsoever of himself before we were adopted together, but he likes the stories I tell him about us. Like the little Grumpy Care Bear he tried to carry around every where he went, or how his hair used to be extremely blond and very curly, and combined with his freckles, how everyone who saw him thought he was the cutest little boy ever.

I think Jerry and I were pretty smart. He was put up for adoption a full two years before me, and yet every time I saw him I whispered to him to tell any prospective families that he didn't want to be adopted without his sister, and that we were a package deal. We concocted plans to say that because I was bigger and older, I'd be out on my own soon, and that I could help them watch Jerry. We took it for granted that Jerry was such a cute little boy that he'd be adopted right away. It was important to us that we were treated as a family and needed to be together. Jerry's stubbornness and my bossiness paid off that time. We were placed in our parents' foster home at the ages of thirteen and ten, with the understanding it was their intention to adopt us. Originally we were set to be adopted by another couple, but they decided they only wanted me, and I was too stubborn in my need to be with my brother to take them seriously.

Our adoptive parents partly adopted us because it was a sign. My name fit theirs perfectly, and my brother had the same name as a father and grandfather. They said they fell in love with us in our adoption video, and also saw Jerry's really cute ad in the newspaper. Our parents had a lot to deal with in adopting two older children. I was completely wild, a street kid, and my brother's temper erupted often. As a whole, our adoption was a huge success, and Jerry and I were very happy to be reunited.

As an adult, Jerry is my hero. I have seen him literally give both his last dollar, and the shirt off his back, to help someone else. He is by far the kindest man I have ever met. Even when he has nothing, he'll give anything he does have. I feel like my brother is an example among men. He has never let a single person down, and when circumstances make it too hard to help someone else, he worries about that person incessantly, and prays that he'll be in a position to help them soon. He's very loyal and very cheerful, and has the biggest heart.

Today there is a new chapter in the history of Rose & Jerry, and it's called ART. My undergraduate degree was from the University of Michigan in English, and my master's work was in Nonprofit Management. Never once did I seriously consider pursuing art because art, to me, was something sacred that was for people who were born with this magical gift. A foster kid wasn't one of those "special ones." Then I found a great book called *The Artist Within* by Julia Cameron, and I followed this workbook for the entire duration of its scope. In this book I learned to not focus on outcomes, but to simply try it, and not fear messing up. This book changed both my brother's life and my own.

Although I live in New Mexico now, I have shown some of my art pieces in downtown Detroit, and have even sold some, but the biggest gift that book gave me was not just inspiring me, but also giving me the tools to inspire my brother and give him a lifelong legacy .

When he tells the story of how he became an artist at the age of twenty-five, Jerry tells this story differently than I do, and it's much bigger and funnier (and this story is another one of the Rose & Jerry legends in its own right.) Jerry's version of the story usually starts off claiming I got him drunk, pushed him from an airplane with a paintbrush in his hand, targeted it specifically so that he would land perfect on a blank sheet of canvas. Or something like that—sometimes I might have forced him to get on a ship and he got seasick and between throwing up... etc., etc. (My brother is a sweetheart, but the average Joe isn't going to match him for creativity!)

The true story is that very few people have believed in Jerry and encouraged him. I have done this to the best of my ability all my life, but I am only one person. That infamous night, I invited Jerry over, and told him we were going to be painting—just him and me. He told me he couldn't paint, and like the bossy older sister I am, I told him I didn't care, that he was going to come over and do it anyway. That night we sat down together, laughed and joked, and amazingly, Jerry started painting something incredible. From his very first painting, my brother proved to be an incredible artist.

Today, Jerry is almost thirty, and has recently started college at the Center for Creative Studies in Michigan for his bachelors. He has about three more years to go, but last year he won a place as one of the best artists in the state of Michigan, and one of his paintings went on tour throughout the state. He works full time to go to school at CCS, and life is still tough for him, but Jerry's story is an amazing one. He has taken the worst of all beginnings, and is turning it around to literally paint a brighter future for himself. I would not want to live in a world without my brother, because I believe it is a better place with people like him in it.

I wish all of you foster children out there who are reading this book could all meet him, really meet him, because I believe you would love him as much as I do. I am so grateful that even through our hard experiences in foster care, we were never truly separated. I am grateful that Jerry and I had a chance to become a real family.

KIMBERLY BROWN-RILEY

Kimberly Brown-Riley entered foster care at the age of one. Though she only lived in one foster home, she still battled the stigma of being a foster child. She says: "I mistakenly allowed what people did around me to influence my perception of myself. So for years I felt that I was worthless, a victim, and had little respect for myself because of what my mother did in her life." Kimberly persevered, eventually overcoming her doubts about herself as a foster child. She was awarded a Department of Children and Family Service scholarship which paid all of her college fees plus provided her with a monthly stipend and medical insurance. Well accomplished, she was also selected to speak at a campaign on Capitol Hill about foster care issues and is also a McNair Scholar. A participant in the Foster Youth Seen and Heard (FYSH) program at the University of Illinois, Kimberly has found comfort in her situation as a former foster child, by writing about her feelings in the program. In discovering herself, she has also discovered that she can be an example to other former foster children. In her essay, "...And Nothing Else and Nothing More," she explores her journey in finding herself, and in "September 1986," she dramatizes herself as a one-year-old child entering foster care for the first time, and how that affected the people around her. For children currently in the system, she says: "I would like to not only say, but be the model and proof to foster children, that you can be very successful in life regardless of the hand you have been dealt. You have to believe in yourself when no one else does, and defend yourself when no one else will. Just know always and remember always that there will be a tomorrow."

...AND NOTHING ELSE AND NOTHING MORE

BY KIMBERLY BROWN-RILEY

"You so funny, girl...You're an unfortunate person...You so ghetto...I bet you are one of them smart girls...Why you got to be so evil?... YouBlack YouGirl YouPoor YouSmart YouDumb YouFOSTERCHILD..."

Out of all of my names, titles and identities, "foster child" hurts the most—my biggest secret—my biggest shame. It meant that I was unwanted. I was a foster child. I was money for someone: their light bill, and or a portion of their mortgage. But me, myself, was NOTHING, nothing but an outcast of an already oppressed group of people, the bottom of an already marginalized group. No other stereotype brought as much pain to me as this name, this identity. I mean, I could talk about sexism with my feminine rights teacher and I could talk about racism with my racial equality preacher, but "foster carism" was an accepted stigma that everyone participated in. I had no one to talk to, so I kept it my secret of secrets.

My friends didn't know, however, the teachers and the preachers did know and they knew also that this meant that I was destined for destruction. No matter how many A's I received or scriptures I memorized, I was a drug baby, the daughter of sin. And this sin was unforgivable. It must have been, because I was constantly reminded of my parents' flaws, but now they were dead. So who would repent for their sins, release me from these titles? Who would tell the pastors that the apple *can* fall far from the tree and that a "bad" tree can bear good fruits? Who would tell my teachers that nurture can impact way more than nature, and that the statistics don't necessarily mean that I am more likely to fail in life? My life shouldn't be a gamble. My potentials shouldn't be minimized. I have no reason to look to the past. In fact, I have forgotten most of it. Now the future isn't worth thinking of, especially when everyone else has predicted it for you.

So now all I have is my life, my present, and my titles. I am a former foster child now. I now carry both my biological name as well as the last name of my adopted family. Even after the adoption, I still experienced life as a foster child. My mom still received checks because of me. There were still foster siblings being placed and removed from my home. I still had a secret to keep. This situation is as uncomfortable as gays living in a homophobic world or blacks living in a racist world. I was a foster youth in a "normal" world. I couldn't tell my secrets because if I did, I would have to defend myself even more because by saying I am a foster youth, I am saying to them that I am on drugs, a thief, will become pregnant as a teen, or will be a juvenile delinquent. If I was a foster youth, according to statistics, I was not to be trusted. I was not to be defended...

I am already a part of a suppressed, underprivileged group of people. How could I be the victim of these victims, their bottom outcast? How could I walk through my high school hallways and overhear my peers bashing foster kids, even though these words were coming from some of the worst kids in school? They'd talk about the lack of potential foster youth have. I'd always want to yell at them: "HOW DARE YOU!!! I never once got in trouble in school unlike you!!!! I am nicer than you, brighter, you are my friend...how could you hurt me?" But they don't know my secrets and I keep it that way. My lips say nothing. I don't stand up. I stay defenseless as always. Given the opportunity to defend myself, I do nothing because I don't know what to do. I am clueless, I can't do what I don't understand. I can't want what I never saw.

In those years during high school, I didn't want to change the world. I only wanted to survive it. And to survive it more comfortably, I had to deny the truth of myself. I had too many other stereotypes to fight. Poor-Black-Female-Inner-City-Youth. Claiming the title "foster child" on top of all of this was another burden I'd decided to escape because it was easy. I didn't have to tell anyone, and therefore didn't have to wear the label. Unfortunately, keeping this secret only made me be dishonest with pieces of myself I should have embraced. I could only openly talk and discuss parts of my identity—not all. Therefore, I never had a positive conversation about myself as a former foster youth and the identities tied to it. These parts of me were never confronted until I became a part of Project FYSH program at the University of Illinois where I had *open* discussions with other youths similar to me, but I was still able to hold onto my own uniqueness. A brick was finally lifted off my shoulders during this time. I could finally introduce myself without fear of stereotypes, but rather receive understanding from the listener. I never knew I could feel this way about myself. All I would have to say from this point on will be "Hi, my name is KIM"... and nothing else and nothing more.

SEPTEMBER 1986

By Kimberly Brown-Riley

Laying face up I begin to cry...

Mom hears my little sister's cry. "Maria," she calls as I come answering to my name grabbing the baby bottle she gives me for my baby sis, Kimberly. She's two years younger than me, I'm almost three and my brother is five. His name is Shaun, he is at my uncle's house. My older sister Erica is at Grandmom's. She is seven, she has MS, she can't walk. "Here, gives this bottle to Kimberly and shut her up," my mom says, emphasizing that latter half of the sentence. The bottle is nearly empty, but it's okay, I know what to do. I climb the top of the toilet with the bottle in my hand, twisting the faucet to pour water in the bottle 'til it fills. Mom walks past the bathroom, sees me, takes the bottle from me. As I climb down, Mom tightens the top for me. She shakes it and pushes the bottle into my chest as I walk out of the bathroom. Kim is still crying, she sounds tired. She is on a blanket between a pillow and the wall. Our house is small, but a lot of people come over, sometimes people sleep with my mom. Sometimes we spend the night with Grandmom. Grandmom lets me help her around the house. I like doing chores. My mom lets me help out a lot, too, but sometimes she screams at me. She screams at all of us. I put the bottle in Kim's mouth, she coughs. I take it out and wait to put it back in...

Crying and screaming, I am helpless...

My sister cries all the time. "Kim, shut up, bitch. ...Maria, come and shut your sister up!" Mom says. I come in, the baby bottle is in the corner. I grab it and rush to the bathroom as Mom leaves the house saying, "I am going out for a smoke. Your sister betta be damn near quiet when I get back or ELSE!"

On top of the toilet, I climb to fill the bottle, but the water won't stay. It is leaking, Kim won't shut up. I know Mom will be mad, I remember Mom threw a shoe at her. It hit her head and she was bleeding. "Kim, be quiet," I say as I drag her to the bathroom. There are no dishes and no food that I can find. I cup my hand in the toilet to give her water, she don't know how to drink it. I get some chicken bones from the garbage to scrape the meat off as I start chewing the gum I find. She won't eat the food, she drools it back out. "Why won't you shut up, Kim?" I ask. She needs to be good, or else. She can't protect herself like me. She is defenseless against the men, too. I sleep with the knives I steal, I hide the keys at night, too. I get whippings from it, but I don't want to die.

Mom is back. She says, "Kim, you still bitchin'. Like my mom says, 'I brought you into this world and I'll take you out." Mom is grabbing Kim by her leg as Kim cries harder. She goes to the stove. "Leave my sister alone, BITCH. Leave her alone, Mommy!!!!!" The stove is on, blue flames, Kim screams as my mom grips on Kim's right leg with both hands. Kim is dying, I know. I am crying. "HELP!!!! SOMEBODY, HELP!!" My legs and hands swing at Mom as my uncle comes in my house. My sister is still crying as she is being taken away from Mom.

I am sleeping in an all-white room. I am warm and feel better...

Why would someone do that to their own child? This is one of the worst cases I've seen and I have been working here for fifteen years as a nurse. "Baby Kim, sleep, sleep the pain away." She had to be treated for third-degree burns, stitches for her forehead that were overdue, malnutrition, and had to be given antibiotics. "We can make you better, just let us take care of you." She is so very small. She was premature and is still small because of malnutrition. She is a fighter. Keep fighting. We give a medical report to the hospital's social worker; we know she has been abused sexually, too. She was dealt a bad hand. Her records from birth show that her mom was doing drugs while pregnant, alcohol, too. It'll be a miracle if she comes out normal. Hopefully, her mother will pay for what her crackhead ass did! She needs to be locked up.

Trees move and the sun follows me...

I sign the paper to check Kimberly out of the hospital.....All of her siblings were taken from their mother. According to files, the father the two youngest shared is dead. The family refuses to take them in and the ones that want to take them in don't qualify. At least the oldest child is staying with the family. The grandma is taking care of her. She has MS and is disabled, mentally and physically. The grandma says she doesn't want another "problem child." Does she think her grandkids will become devils just because her daughter made some mistakes? Whatever. I found a home for the two girls, Kim and Maria. A new foster mother, a woman who raised both of her sons to adulthood. She says she always wanted girls. She doesn't take in their brother, no matter how much I beg. Her house is nice. Clean. She seems nice. She is forty-nine and just took in her first foster child, a little two-year-old girl. She is brave. She will be taking care of a one-year-old, two-year-old and three-year-old. All credits to her.

The doctors finally give me Kim, and I carry her to my car, placing her in the car seat. Today, traffic is light so I look over at Kim a couple of times. She doesn't make noise, not once the whole ride, but just stares through the window at the sky and scenery. Her sister is already at the house. I am sure she will smile when she is reunited with her.

I remain quiet...

Maria is so wild. They say that it is normal because of her age and plus 'cause of what she's been through. I know that I am new with this foster care business, but next time that girl takes one of my knives and takes it in the bed with her, I am going to whip her like it is no tomorrow. That girl scares me. I'm glad her sister is a baby, still, I couldn't handle two of them. The two-year-old girl, Evelyn, doesn't talk or walk. Her father threw her down the stairs and made her braindamaged. The doctor says she will never walk or talk but I know that there is nothing impossible for God. I am going to pray for that girl.

...Ding-dong..."Maria, you betta sit down and behave while I answer this door," I say. Where is that girl getting all that energy from, she must be steal-

ing candy from somewhere. She bet not be stealing my Sweetlow sugar, that's for my diabetes.

"Hi, Mrs. Halls, and this must be Kim." She is so small, she doesn't respond to my touch, not even to flinch. She just stares at me with her eyes wide open, looking through me, I guess.....

...I'll pray for her, too.

IN THE BEGINNING...

In closing out this book, I've decided to end with the story that started me on this journey. While pursuing my master's degree, I was challenged to write a group of essays surrounding one pivotal experience in my life. Pushed to dig deep and write about something personal yet painful, I first chose to share my foster care experience with my class. Though I later moved on to another topic, the assignment awoke in me the need to share my story, and seek out other stories like mine that I felt were not being shared. This essay was originally written in the year 2000, so although some of the facts and statistics have changed, my need to show that not all foster kids perish in the system has not. I appreciate your support in reading this book, and I hope you will enjoy this final essay, the one that started it all.

THE PRIDE OF FOSTER CARE

BY CHARISSE NESBIT

Walking past a newsstand one day in November 2000 I saw something that stopped me in my tracks. On the stand was a *Time* magazine cover with a picture of a little boy who was naked from the waist up. The expression on his face was that of resignation and self-pity. Small spots from healing bruises could be seen on his emaciated chest and his head leaned back over one shoulder as he peered pathetically at the camera. I recognized the boy immediately as I'd seen his picture before in another such article in another magazine months earlier. Below the picture in large letters were the words: "The Shame of Foster Care." The story was not new, and my frustration with the subject matter wasn't, either. Despite this I purchased the magazine to see what new accusations were being thrown about and what new solutions, if any, would be offered.

Upon reading the story, I was treated with horror stories of neglected and abused children broken down into three states: Georgia, Alabama, and California. The story starts right in with the sight of the boy's dead body on the autopsy table. "A hospital tube protrudes from his broken nose. He has deep cuts above his right ear and dark linear scars on his forehead...Little Terrell Peterson had so many injuries that the medical examiner gave up counting them...He weighed only 29 lbs. The foster-care system is not working in Atlanta (*Time* 74)." The stories went on to include deaths in Chicago and Wyoming in addition to the states listed above. I had to admit the stories were horrific and the neglect by the system inexcusable, but I was still angry at the article. In the five pages it covered, the only light offered was a small insert of about three kids who had managed to make it out of the system. While the article pointed out the system's atrocities, it offered absolutely no solutions to the problems, and very little in the way of kids who actually managed to make it out of the system not only alive, but also successful, productive members of American society.

As a product of the foster care system myself, I was deeply affected by the article and saddened that no solutions were offered. Although I was angered enough to produce an idea to deal with this problem with my pen, until now I have yet to take that first step to change people's perceptions of foster kids. For just about all of my life I have avoided talking about my own experience because of other's misconceptions and immediate pity. Though I was considered a ward of the court, I am one of the many lucky survivors of the system who not only got out un-scathed, but even better for the experience. I really feel that without foster care, I wouldn't be where I am today. Through my research for this paper, I have managed to uncover several other people, most of them very well known, who would more than likely agree with that sentiment. I'd mentioned earlier about my neglect to take the first step to answer those who criticize the foster care system and write all of its products off as hopeless, wayward children. So here it is. My first step.

Enter the words "foster care" into a library search engine, and imme-diately you get titles such as: "Can this child be saved?" or "What child is this?" or "Orphans of the Living: The Children of America's Foster Care System." Visions of indigent, abused, and neglected children auto-matically follow. Add to this mix a bevy of magazine articles, books, and television magazine specials detailing the many sad stories of the American foster care system, and the average person reading these stories is led to believe that there is very little hope for the average child in foster care. Obviously Travis Butler of East Memphis, Tennessee heard some of these stories. In the December/January 1999-2000 issue of *Jet* magazine, it was reported that the boy lived with his dead mother for a month because he was afraid of being placed into foster care. The boy went so far as to bathe himself, cut his hair, and even signed his mother's name quite convincingly to school reports to cover up her death. All because he was afraid of being placed into the foster care system. A family friend, Dorothy Jeffries, finally found Travis alone in the apartment with the dead body covered in his mother's coat with notebook paper over her face. "I just don't know how that baby survived in there for a month with that smell...It was the saddest thing I have ever seen in my life," she said.

Travis' apprehension isn't without merit. The foster care system is far from perfect, and unfortunately there are some sad stories to be told: infants beaten to death or drowned in toilets, children starved within an inch of their lives; but contrary to popular belief, there are some positive stories as well. Some of the names connected to these stories would no doubt surprise you. In fact, there are many famous and successful people who were once a part of the system. Judges, governors, actors, politicians, writers, and the list goes on.

Some of these people were educated by money provided by this system, or given a home they may not have had otherwise. Many have experienced the neglect of parents, and the endless string of different homes, families, and situations, but they have managed to become successful nonetheless. These are the stories you rarely hear whenever foster care is mentioned, although some of the names I will mention in this paper will be very familiar. Unfortunately, though the positive achievements of these people are highly recognized, the fact that foster care was involved in their upbringing and at times even contributed to their success is often omitted from the stories. While distressing stories may sell more papers or magazines, everyone reading these stories needs to know some of the positive aspects of the foster care system, as well as the names of some of the people who are better for having been a part of it.

As of April 2001, the number of children removed from their birth homes and placed into foster care numbered about 568,000 (76-77, *Harpers*). More than a fifth of these children were slated for permanent adoption (76-77). Many of these children are neglected—abandoned by roadsides, starved to death, abused. Once dropped into the foster care system, they are sometimes forgotten, shuffled through the court system, passed back and forth between multiple homes, or sometimes if they are older children, placed in a home for children in crisis like Miss Teen USA 1992, Charlotte Ayanna. Ayanna, whose birth name was Charlotte Lopez before she changed it after finding out Ayanna was the name of the grandfather who abandoned her mother, spent time in five different foster homes before the age of fourteen. One of the homes kept her for eleven years but did not adopt her. Ayanna then ended up at the group home where she did very well in school and went on to win Miss Teen USA in 1992. Ayanna is now an author and an actress, but what I remember most is her victory that night. Watching her from my own foster home where I lived from the age of seven to twenty-one, I was very proud of her. In the small town where I grew up, everyone knew that my "aunt" was really my foster mother, but it was never spoken about. It was always treated as a shameful thing, especially since my mother and the rest of my family were very much alive and even involved in my life through monthly visits. As I watched the then Charlotte Lopez proudly proclaim that she was a foster child, it made me wonder why it was such a shameful thing for me to admit to many of my friends at school. If she could do it on national television and not only not get ridiculed for it but prosper and win a national contest, what was I afraid of? I continued on with life after that moment a little prouder of who I was and what life for me as a foster child meant, but I still kept it to myself. Still, positive images of foster children such as Charlotte Lopez made me feel a little better, and taught me that nothing I wanted was out of my reach just because of my background.

Unfortunately, as I mentioned earlier, stories such as Charlotte's are few and far between, but not because they don't exist. They are just not spoken of often. Because of the stigma attached to foster care, and because we are thought of as "nobody's children," it is no wonder that many famous people are rarely revealed as former foster children.

I'm sure everyone is aware of Eddie Murphy through his countless movies, albums, comedy shows, and television appearances, but I'm equally as sure that not many people realize that he was also once a foster child.

Eddie Murphy's father was killed when he was very young, and his mother, who was often sick and sometimes unable to care for him, had to hand him over to the foster care system. Though it's not clear how long he spent in the system, it is clear that he went on to become very successful, getting discovered at the age of nineteen in a comedy club, and becoming an international star by the age of twenty-one. While the foster care system can't exactly take the full credit for his success, some credit is due: it was there to take care of him until his mother could get back on her feet and properly care for her son herself. It also gave us one of the most popular and talented entertainers today.

Along with these former foster kids, are two that are recognized as true icons. The first is Marilyn Monroe, born to a single mother in 1926 when it was taboo to have children out of wedlock. Her father walked out on Marilyn's pregnant mother and never met her. Overwhelmed with single parenthood, Marilyn's mother put her in a foster home where she stayed for seven years. Her mother continued to visit her every weekend and when she reached the age of eight, returned to her mother who had purchased a small house.

From there Marilyn was raised by her mother where she stayed for a year until it was made clear her mother was insane. Marilyn was raised briefly by a lady she called "Aunt Grace" until she was removed from her home. She then was placed in an orphanage from the ages of nine to eleven when she was placed back with "Aunt Grace." At fifteen she had the alternative to either get married to her boyfriend or go back to the orphanage, so she chose to get married. By the time she was twenty, she divorced her husband and was well on her way to super stardom.

Marilyn Monroe is best known for dozens of publicity photos, as well as movies such as *Some Like it Hot* and *Gentlemen Prefer Blondes*. She isn't as well known for being a foster child. It also isn't known that for all of the turbulence in her life, her time spent in foster care was the longest time she'd spent in any sort of home environment. Most likely it was the most normal family situation she'd had, although her foster family was very strict and religious. While her life was not perfect by any means, it is clear that she too benefited from the service that foster care provides. Her mother chose a foster home that would be close to her grandmother, but had she been left in the care of her grandmother instead of foster care, she may not have survived to become the star we all know of today. Marilyn claimed that she had memories as an infant of being strangled by her grandmother. Her grandmother was later committed to an insane asylum, so it is believed that this claim is true. Foster care may have its horror stories, but there are some kids who have managed to survive the system, and even those who have survived because of it.

Along with lawyers, beauty queens, and movie stars, there are also people in the political arena who have benefited from foster care. Perhaps the most famous of these is Malcolm X. Malcolm X was born Malcolm Little in 1925. His father, a Baptist minister and outspoken supporter of Marcus Garvey, a Black Nationalist leader, was murdered when Malcolm was a child. His mother was committed to an insane asylum and Malcolm and his seven siblings were all sent to different foster homes. Malcolm was a prolific student and did very well in school despite discouragement from his teachers. He later ran away and fell into a life of crime, selling and using marijuana and cocaine. He was arrested and sent to prison in Boston in 1946.

While in prison Malcolm learned of the Muslim religion. He became a devout follower and upon his release from prison, he threw himself wholeheartedly into his religion. He rose through the ranks of the Nation of Islam and was soon ordained a minister and given a position at a Detroit mosque. He also studied privately under Elijah Muhammad and was sent to Philadelphia to set up a new congregation. Malcolm X soon became a leader of the Nation of Islam and its mouthpiece to the nation. Malcolm X is a sometimes controversial figure, but like him or not, he was a very successful and powerful leader in the Muslim community. Despite all of the ups and downs in his life, he managed to overcome a hard beginning and tough times and persevere to become one of the most recognizable names and faces in American politics today.

Among all of the people mentioned above, there are several more famous people who were at one time foster children. A few of these include actress Victoria Rowell, Dr. Ruth Westheimer, comedian Tommy Davidson, Babe Ruth, rapper Ice T, John Lennon, James Dean, and Eleanor Roosevelt, among others. In the midst of all of the bad and down-and-out stories about foster care, it is important to recognize those who have managed to beat the odds and make it through the system to become fully realized and successful adults. For every bad story there is at least one good one, and it is about time that people recognize this and give hope to those foster kids still in the system, so they won't end up thinking of themselves as "nobody's child."

I would be remiss in this paper if I didn't mention at least part of my own experience with foster care. I will be first to admit that my experience was not necessarily typical of most kids in foster care. Foster care is meant to be a temporary fix with the purpose of either reuniting a child with their families, or at least finding them an adoptive family. When my three brothers, one sister and I were placed in a foster home, we were told we would be there for six months. At the time, I had no idea what six months meant. I only knew that it was not supposed to be a long time, just until my mother could get herself on her feet, but that would never happen. I entered the home with my siblings when I was seven years old and remained there until the age of eighteen, still coming back to stay periodically on trips home from college until the age of twenty-one.

First of all, I was fortunate that I was able to be placed with all of my siblings. My older brother only stayed about a year, managing to leave and find refuge with my grandmother. The rest of us stayed much longer, with my sister leaving once she turned eighteen to attend a trade school and then the army, and my twin brother leaving to live with my grandmother and later my mother at about sixteen when he was drafted to play football for a local private school. My younger brother left when he was about sixteen, also going to live with my grandmother, and I stayed through all of it. For me, I saw no need to leave. Foster care was not an ideal situation as we were always aware that we were not blood relatives, but it was better than a single-parent home where my mother worked three jobs just to survive.

Within foster care, I was provided with a home and structure and given opportunities I would not have had otherwise. Early on it was discovered that I needed glasses which I got, though they were not the latest style or even stylish at all. Later I got braces which I desperately needed and would probably not have gotten had I not been in foster care. The Medicare benefits I received as a foster child paid for what otherwise would have been a very expensive procedure—definitely more than my family could have handled on our own.

Foster care also provided me with an education. Wanting to get out and see another part of the country, I chose to attend school at the University of New Mexico. Through foster care I received a grant which helped me pay part of my tuition, as well as my foster mother's monthly stipend for me which paid for my room and board. Because I was considered a ward of the court, I was declared independent which allowed me to receive the maximum amount of financial aid. Had I not been a ward of the court, I would have undoubtedly received much less and would have had to rely more on loans to pay for my education. Being independent and declaring my residency in New Mexico after a year, combined with the lowered cost of tuition as a result, I owed very little in student loans by the time my tenure was up at The University of New Mexico. Had it not been for the financial help I received as well as the guidance from my social worker in helping me find a college, I may never have gone at all. More than likely, I would have become a statistic rather than a person with her Bachelor's degree and now a candidate for a graduate degree.

Even with all of the help that I received from foster care, because of the stigma attached to it, I have kept my affiliation with it a secret for the most part. Most of my friends do not even know that I was a foster child. I couldn't stand the thought of the questions that would inevitably come. Where was your mother? Why didn't she take you back? Why didn't the rest of your family help? To be honest I don't know the answer to all of these questions. Many things in my family are not spoken about, which is why I keep certain things like my time in foster care private. Hiding things about myself became a way of life as I grew older and had to fend for myself more and more. Teasing classmates and horror stories like that of Brianna Blackmond, who died in December 2000 at the hands of her slightly retarded mother after being removed from foster care, served to keep my mouth shut. Everything I'd heard about foster care and the children within it was negative and I didn't want that picture painted of me as well. I didn't want the pitying looks and the *tsk-tsks* that I was sure would come if I revealed I was a former foster child.

Even with my first big success as a writer, when an essay I wrote, "Child of the Dream," appeared in a national publication with quotes from my essay all over the book—on the back cover, the inside cover, and the introduction—one thing was missing. It was the fact that mostly everything I talked about in the essay had occurred during my stint in foster care. I spoke of my identity crisis of growing up black in a country that didn't always accept me, as well as my own problems with identities within my race. I told of how I found myself in Atlanta and finally felt comfortable in my own skin, and how I continue to grow with every endeavor, but I still didn't talk about the role foster care had in this growth. By hiding this part of me I was not telling the whole story, and I not only did my readers a disservice, but myself and my foster mother and father as well. While I was always aware that I would never be loved like one of their own, my foster parents were the closest thing to a real family I had for a while, and overall, there was love on both sides.

My foster parents gave me and my siblings a very strong upbringing in the church. We went every Sunday, and sometimes even during the week. We had square meals, and while my foster mother, who was older and used to doing without much was frugal, we had clothes and shoes. Not always the latest style, but we had what we needed. Most of all, we had a structure to our lives. Something that we hadn't had before foster care. Something that we may not have had without it. Because my mother and her side of the family were still in my life, I feel I got the best of both worlds. Time with my mother was always fun and frivolous, and I was exposed to things that I wouldn't have gotten in the small country town where my foster mother lived. My mother always lived close to a city like Baltimore, Maryland, or Wilmington, Delaware. Her friends were fun and interesting: roller skaters and dancers full of wild stories and good times, champagne in fancy glasses and exotic foods. In my foster mother's house we usually ate mashed potatoes, chicken, fish, corn, or whatever my foster father grew in his garden. Later on we'd mostly dine on easy-to-prepare frozen foods bought from the local low-cost meat store.

Throughout my entire experience, I never really realized how fortunate I was to have been in foster care. Looking back now, I do. The structure and discipline it gave me throughout my life have been unparalleled. Because of the experience, it has allowed me to realize my own dreams and push me to make them come true. This outcome is different than a great deal of foster children leaving the system. According to an April 2001 article in *The Education Digest*, forty-five percent of kids in foster care become homeless within a year, and a third of children in foster care overall eventually become homeless (66). It also said that thirty percent of foster children are likely to become substance abusers, and fifty percent may lose one or more of their own children to the system (66). Once again, I am faced with the overwhelmingly bad numbers of the outcome of kids recovering from their time in foster care, but I am content in the knowledge that I am not one of them. So far I have managed to beat the odds, and I know I will continue to do so. As I've said before, if it weren't for foster care, I may never have gone to college. I shudder to think where I may have gone instead. I look at the people I grew up with who had two-parent homes and more often than not, they are still where they were when we left high school. Ultimately, it is up to each individual to carve out his or her own destiny, but help and guidance along the way certainly doesn't hurt.

My siblings also have managed to fair quite well despite our upbringing in the system. My sister does probation on a national level and turned down a position in the FBI to instead stay in our home state and have a life of her own. She is now married with her first child, Sydnee (she has since had another child, Joshua), who is eight months old. My older brother is a supervisor at his job and is raising his two children on his own. A third lives with her mother and visits on the weekends. My younger brother is currently in transition after leaving the army where he was a sergeant. He is currently starting his life over on the outside and is using the skills he learned in the army to hold down a job as an operating room technician. He has four children. My twin brother is a vice president at a bank and has been there for over ten years, becoming an executive at the age of twenty-four. He has one child as well. I am the only one without a child, by choice, thus far, but my siblings all have made that choice, and they are living up to it and taking care of their responsibilities as parents. Despite our displacement, we've managed to keep the children of our family as a priority. Education has also become a priority with us. With the exception of my younger brother who went into the army right out of high school, we all have our undergraduate degrees with my twin brother holding the only master's among us (for now). I am very proud that we all have managed to prosper and become very successful in spite of statistics which say it should have been otherwise.

We are all examples that it is not where you come from, but where you're going that matters. Unfortunately, our stories are not always told in the media as a whole. Instead kids like us currently in the system are force-fed stories of the horrors of foster care, and led to believe that they are "nobody's child," or "anybody's child." They are rarely encouraged to do more and be more, because stories of destitute poverty and horrific abuse sell more papers than those of the children who managed to overcome and persevere beyond their humble beginnings. This is something that must change, and hopefully with this paper, I'm making my first step in the right direction to be a part of that process.

Along with my meager effort however, there are more positive changes affected recently that will give newer foster care children a better chance and hope for the future. The Adoption and Safe Families Act (AFSA) of 1997 was enacted by Congress as an amendment to an earlier act, the Adoption Assistance and Child Welfare Act (AACWA) which unfortunately missed its mark to help families. The goal of the AFSA was to double the number of foster children being adopted by this year. This law was set in place to speed up the procedures in place to get foster children into adoptive families. This act was fueled by negative press which focused on the horrors of foster care. Thus the AFSA was also set up to ensure a child's safety over parental rights, which was a big problem with the AACWA. The AFSA, by focusing on adoption, hopes to ensure a better family life and more stability for the children it affects. As the program is still relatively new, the overall effects thus far are not certain. Though there have been critics of this program, of the articles that I've read regarding the horror stories of foster care, most of the fatalities I read about occurred because the children were placed back with parents who weren't equipped to handle them, and not because of foster care. The AFSA understands this phenomenon and in certain cases, even allows for a parent's rights to be permanently terminated. While there is a possibility for error here, overall, I feel it is a positive step in the direction of helping more of the biggest victims of these situations, the children, finally find a place to call home.

Here in Chicago, the group One Church One Child, in place since 1980, did its part in finding adoptive homes for children in foster care, resulting in the placement of over 90,000 children into adoptive homes by 1998. One Church One Child works with placing African-American children into African-American adoptive homes, sometimes even the homes of church members themselves. While this is sometimes a controversial method, keeping African-American children with those of their own race, it has been highly successful in this program, and continues to be successful today.

Bringing the face of foster care into the new millennium are internet homepages which act like a surrogate orphanage for "waiting children." Most of the children featured on sites such as these have been "freed" for adoption, meaning their parents' rights have been terminated, usually due to problems of abuse. The websites offer options such as narrowing your search by age, gender, and race, among other things. They are up-front about the child's emotional problems or challenges due to mistreatment or concern over their own well-being. Profiles of each child are usually written by the child's social worker. These sites are still new, and there are more in the making, so the success rate is still in limbo as well. With the easy accessibility of the child's picture, as well as his or her background all available with the click of a mouse, hopefully this newest advancement in the placement of children will work in getting more children into waiting, loving homes.

One of the most surprising developments in the advancement of improving foster care has come in the force of President George W. Bush's budget breakdown of March 2001, as provided by the Associated Press. In it Bush proposed to offer $60 million for education and training vouchers for children "graduating" out of the foster care system by turning eighteen. These vouchers would help these children obtain an education by giving them assistance for college tuition or for vocational schools. Each of the vouchers could be worth up to $5,000. The budget breakdown also allots $505 million to assist states in investigating child abuse and neglect claims, as well as removing them from abusive homes and placing them in more protective homes. These proposals have yet to take effect to my knowledge, but the provision to include them in the budget for our nation is definitely a step in the right direction.

From the good to the bad to the ugly, the foster care system definitely has its ups and downs, as does anything in this world. There are obviously some things about foster care that can be changed and improved upon. As I've stated, there are gestures being made to enact changes. The most positive change would be to focus on the positive aspects of the system and to enact changes within it. Pointing fingers and accusing words won't bring a child back, and they won't save the next child until some action to change things is backing up those words. As a product of the system, I am proof that some good can come of it, and that there is also hope for other children currently in the system.

WORKS CITED

1. Bagwell, Jodi. "Foster Kids: Nurturing 'Anybody's Child.'" *The Education Digest*. v. 66 no 8. Pgs. 63-66. April 2001.

2. Moore, Art. "Can Foster Care Be Fixed?" *Christianity Today*. v. 42 no. 9. Pgs. 54-57. August 1998.

3. Roche, Timothy. "The Crisis of Foster Care." *Time*. v. 156 no. 20. Pgs. 74-82. November 2000.

4. Higham, Scott, and Horwitz, Sari. "Brianna, Buried in System's Mistakes." *The Washington Post*. Pg. A01. December 2000.

5. Foster Club authors. "Charlotte Ayanna: Ms. Teen USA, Author, Actress, and a Foster Kid." www.fosterclub.com. January 2002.

6. Foster Club authors. "Marilyn Monroe: Movie Star Legend and a Foster Kid." www.fosterclub.com. January 2002.

7. Foster Club authors. "Eddie Murphy...Actor, Funnyman, and a Foster Kid." www.fosterclub.com. January 2002.

8. Foster Club authors. "Malcolm X." www.fosterclub.com. January 2002.

9. *Jet* editors. "Boy Fearing Foster Care, Lived With Mother's Corpse for a Month." *Jet*. v. 97 no. 3. Pgs. 13-14. December 1999-January 2000.

10. *People* editors. "Losing Her Children." *People Weekly*. v. 56 no. 3 Pg. 57. Time Inc. July 2001.

11. Farber, Peggy. "Broken Homepage: Putting a Happy Face on Foster Child Adoption." *Harpers*. v. 302 no. 1811. Pgs. 76-77. April 2001.

12. Stein, Theodore J. "The Adoption and Safe Families Act: Creating a False Dichotomy Between Parents and Childrens' (i.e. Children's) Rights." *Families in Society*. v. 81. no. 6. Pgs. 586-92. November/December 2000.

13. Associated Press editors. "Bush Budget Breakdown." www.archives.seattletimes.nwsource.com. *The Seattle Times* Co. March 2001.

RESOURCES

LIST OF CHILD WELFARE RESOURCES, STATE BY STATE

ALASKA

STATE COORDINATOR(S)
Department of Health and Social Services
Jefty Pranther, IL Coordinator
PO Box 110612,
Juneau, AK 99811
Phone: (907) 465-3235
Email: jeftyp@yahoo.com
Website: www.state.ak.us

Juneau Youth Services
P.O. Box 32839
Juneau, AK 99803
Phone: (907) 789-9103
Phone: (907) 789-9103

Kids Are People, Inc.
Rich McGill
561 West Nelson Avenue
Wasilla, AK 99645
Phone: (907) 376-0740
Email: tlc@kidsarepeople.org
Website: www.kidsarepeople.org

Southcentral Foundation
Arcenio Charleston, TLP Contact
Email: Acharleson@southcentralfoundation.com
4501 Diplomacy Drive, Suite 200
Anchorage, AK 99508
Phone: (907) 729-5239

ALABAMA

STATE COORDINATOR(S)
Alabama Department of Human Resources
Wanda Davidson, IL Program Specialist
50 Ripley Street
Montgomery, AL 36130
Phone: (334) 353-4208
Fax: (334) 353-1491
Email: wanda.davidson@dhr.alabama.gov

Children's Aid Society
Gayle Watts
Melissa Bunch, TLP Contact
181 West Valley Avenue, Suite 300
Homewood, AL 35222
Phone: (205) 251-7148
Fax: (205) 252-3828
Email: mbunch@childrensaid.org
Website: www.childrensaid.org

Tennessee Valley Family Services, Inc.
Michael Thomas, Executive Director
Leslie Putnam, TLP Contact
P.O. Box 952
Guntersville, AL 35976
Phone: (256) 582-0377
Email: tvfstlp@hiwaay.net

ARKANSAS

STATE COORDINATOR(S)
Arkansas Division of Children & Family Services
Jim Dennis, IL Coordinator
700 Main Street
Little Rock, AR 72202
Phone: (501) 682-8453
Fax: (501) 682-8991
Email: james.dennis@arkansas.gov

FYSB FUNDED TRANSITIONAL LIVING PROGRAMS (TLP)
Center for Youth and Families (Stepping Stone)
Doug Stadter, President/CEO
Email: dstadter@aristotle.net
Marvin Taylor, TLP Contact
Email: Mtaylor@aristotle.net
6501 W. 12th St.
Little Rock, AR 72204
Phone: (501) 666-8686
Website: www.youthandfamilies.org

ARIZONA

STATE COORDINATOR(S)
Arizona Department of Economic Security
Beverlee B. Kroll, IL Coordinator
2328 West Guadelupe Road
Gilbert, AZ 85233
Phone: (480) 545-1901
Fax: (480) 926-5161
Email: bkroll@azdes.gov

FYSB FUNDED TRANSITIONAL LIVING PROGRAMS (TLP)
Family Counseling Agency of Tucson, Inc.
Frank Williams, Executive Director
Fred Jacobson, TLP Contact
209 S. Tucson Boulevard, Suite 1
Tucson, AZ 85716
Phone: (520) 327-4583
Email: fca@fcaonline.org

Our Town Family Center
Regina Gillis
Sue Krahe-Eggleston, Executive Director
Email: skrahe@aol.com
3830 East Bellevue Street
Tucson, AZ 85716-4012
Phone: (520) 293-3015
Fax: (520) 323-9077
Email: commonunityotfc@aol.com
Website: www.otfc.org

Tumbleweed Center for Youth
Dick Geasland, Executive Director
Email: rgeasland@tumbleweed.org
Patrick Wood, TLP Contact
Email: woods227@hotmail.com
1419 N. 3rd Street, Suite 102
Phoenix, AZ 85004
Phone: (602) 468-2417
Fax: (602) 956-5623

CALIFORNIA

STATE COORDINATOR(S)
California Department of Social Services
Jill Sevaaetasi
IL Program Policy Unit
744 P Street, M.S. 14-78
Sacramento, CA 95814
Phone: (916) 651-9774
Fax: (916) 657-4357
Email: jsevaaet@dss.ca.gov

FYSB FUNDED TRANSITIONAL LIVING PROGRAMS (TLP)
Bill Wilson Center
Sparky Harlan
3490 The Alameda
Santa Clara, CA 95050
Phone: (408) 243-0222

Center for Human Services
Linda Kovacs
1700 McHenry Village Way
Modesto, CA 95350
Phone: (209) 526-1440
Email: lkovacs@centerforhumanservices.org

Center for Positive Prevention
Alternatives
Linda Mascarenas
729 N. California Street
Stockton, CA 95202
Phone: (209) 929-6700
Email: ljmascarenas@cppainc.org
Website: www.cppainc.org

City of Richmond
Upesi Mtambuzi
330 25th Street
Richmond, CA 94804
Phone: (510) 307-8153

Contra Costa County Health Services
Homeless Program
Lavonna Martin
597 Center Avenue, Ste. 335
Martinez, CA 94553
Phone: (925) 313-6140
Email: lmartin@hsd.co.contra-costa.ca.us
Website: www.cchealth.org

Diogenes Youth Services
James Bureto, TLP Contact
Email: dys9719@sbcglobal.net
9719 Lincoln Village Dr., # 110
Sacramento, CA 95827
Phone: (916) 369-5447
Fax: (916) 369-5389
Email: ys59719@sbcglobal.net
Website: www.diogenesnet.com

Emergency Housing Consortium
Michelle Covert
150 Almaden Avenue, Suite 500
San Jose, CA 95113
Phone: (408) 294-2660
Email: mcovert@homelessness.org
Website: www.homelessness.org

Fresno County Economic Opportunities
Commission Sanctuary Transitional
Living Center
Katrina Edwards
1046 T. Street
Fresno, CA 93721
Phone: (559) 498-8543
Phone: (559) 268-1045
Email: katrina-edwards@fresnoeoc.org
Website: www.fresnoeoc.org

Larkin Street Youth Services
Sherilyn Adams, Executive Director
1138 Sutter Street
San Francisco, CA 94109
Phone: (415) 673-0911
Email: sherilynadams@larkinstreetyouth.org

Los Angeles Conservation Corps
Phil Matero, Executive Director
Reyna Albizures, TLP Contact
3655 Grand Avenue, Suite 280
Los Angeles, CA 90007
Phone: (213) 749-3601
Email: ralbizures@lacorps.org

Mendocino Family and Youth Services
Lyle Coburn
347 A Plum Street
Ukiah, CA 95482
Phone: (707) 462-3354
Fax: (707) 462-3325
Email: lcoburn@mcyp.org
Website: www.mcyp.org

Operation Safehouse
Kathy McAdara
9685 Hayes Street
Riverside, CA 92503
Phone: (951) 351-4418
Email: safehouse9@aol.com
Website: www.operationsafehouse.org

San Diego Youth and Community Services
Annette Mike
3255 Wing Street
San Diego, CA 92110
Phone: (619) 221-8610 ext. 275
Fax: (619) 221-8619
Email: amike@sdycs.org
Website: www.sdycs.org

South Bay Community Services
Trolley Trestle
Jose Montes, TLP Contact
1124 Bay Blvd., Suite D
Chula Vista, CA 91911
Phone: (619) 420-3620
Fax: (619) 420-8722
Email: jmontes@csbcs.org
Website:
www.southbaycommunityservices.org

The Salvation Army
Gabriella Wynn
P.O. Box 38668
Los Angeles, CA 90038
Phone: (323) 469-2946
Email: gabriella_wynn@usw.salvationarmy.org

Waking the Village and Tubman House
Briget Alexander, Executive Director
P.O. Box 459
Herald, CA 95638
Phone: (916) 372-6272
Email: admin@wakingthevillage.org
Website: www.wakingthevillage.org

YMCA of San Diego County
Ken Tyner, Program Director
Laura Mustari, TLP Contact
4080 Centre Street
San Diego, CA 92103
Phone: (619) 543-9850
Email: ktyner@ymca.org

Youth and Family Assistance
Robert Rybicki
610 Elm Street, Suite 212
San Carlos, CA 94070-3070
Phone: (650) 366-8401

**Youth and Family Enrichment Services
Daybreak**
Douglas Styles, TLP Contact
639 Douglas Avenue
Redwood City, CA 94063
Phone: (650) 364-4633
Fax: (650) 369-4584
Email: douglas.styles@yfes.org
Website: www.yfes.org

COLORADO

STATE COORDINATOR(S)
Colorado Department of Human Services, Child Welfare Alive/e Program
Brenda Redding, IL Coordinator
1575 Sherman Street, 2nd Floor
Denver, CO 80203
Phone: (303) 866-4539
Email: Brenda.Redding@state.co.us

FYSB FUNDED TRANSITIONAL LIVING PROGRAMS (TLP)
Urban Peak
Jerene Petersen
1630 South Acoma
Denver, CO 80223
Phone: (303) 777-8082
Email: jerene@urbanpeak.org
Website: www.urbanpeak.org

Volunteers of America
Dianna Kunz, President
1865 Larrimer Street
Denver, CO 80205
Phone: (303) 295-2165
Website: www.voacolorado.org

CONNECTICUT

STATE COORDINATOR(S)
Connecticut Department of Children and Families
Frank Martin, IL Coordinator
505 Hudson Street
Hartford, CT 06106
Phone: (860) 550-6592
Fax: (860) 566-6727
Email: FRANK.MARTIN@po.state.ct.us

FYSB FUNDED TRANSITIONAL LIVING PROGRAMS (TLP)
The Bridge Family Center
Margaret Hann, Executive Director
1022 Farmington Avenue
West Hartford, CT 06107
Phone: (806) 521-8023
Email: margaret@bridgefamilycenter.org
Website: www.bridgefamilycenter.org

Youth Continuum
Carole A. Shomo
746 Chapel Street, 4th floor
New Haven, CT 06510
Phone: (203) 562-3396

DELAWARE

STATE COORDINATOR(S)
Division of Family Services
Truman Bolden, IL Program Manager
1825 Faulkland Road
Wilmington, DE 19805
Phone: (302) 633-2638
Fax: (302) 633-2652
Email: Truman.bolden@state.de.us

FYSB FUNDED TRANSITIONAL LIVING PROGRAMS (TLP)
Aid in Dover
Beverly Williams
838 Walker Road
Dover, DE 19904
Phone: (302) 734-7610
Email: bwilliams@aidindover.org
Website: www.aidindover.org

FLORIDA

STATE COORDINATOR(S)
Florida Department of Children and Families
Joel Atkinson, State IL Program Mgr.
1317 Winewood Boulevard, Bldg. 6
Tallahassee, FL 32399-0700
Phone: (850) 487-2383
Fax: (850) 448-0688
Email: joel_atkinson@dcf.state.fl.us

FYSB FUNDED TRANSITIONAL LIVING PROGRAMS (TLP)
Arnette House
Kevin Priest
2310 NE 24th Street
Ocala, FL 34470
Phone: (352) 622-4432
Fax: (352) 662-2830
Email: kevinpriest@hotmail.com

Children's Home Society
Mary Ellen Maguire
415 Avenue A, Suite 101
Ft. Pierce, FL 34950
Phone: (772) 489-5601 ext. 286
Email: maryellen.maguire@chsfl.org

Children's Home Society
Curt D' Achille
3335 Forest Hill Blvd.
West Palm Beach, FL 33407
Phone: (561) 868-4367
Email: curt.dachille@chsfl.org
Website: www.chsfl.org

Covenant House Florida
Cathy Branch
733 Breakers Avenue
Fort Lauderdale, FL 33304
Phone: (954) 568-7939

Crosswinds Youth Services, Inc.
Jan Lokay
P.O. Box 540625
Merritt Island, FL 32954
Phone: (305) 452-8988
Email: janlokay@crosswindsyouthservices.org

**Family Resources, Inc.
(Residential South)**
Jane Harper, Executive Director
Email: jane@family-resources.org
Jim Welch, TLP Contact
Email: jwelch@family-resources.org
P.O. Box 13087
St. Petersburg, FL 33733
Phone: (813) 341-2200
Fax: (727) 550-4054

**Hillsborough County Child and Family Counseling Program
(Haven W. Poe Runaway Center)**
Barry Drew, Executive Director
Judy Ferlita, TLP Contact
Email: ferlitajd@hillsboroughcounty.org
207 Beach Place
Tampa, FL 33606
Phone: (813) 272-6606

Hillsborough County Department of Children's Services
Susan D. Stagon
3110 Clay Mangum Lane
Tampa, FL 33618
Phone: (813) 264-3807 ext. 163
Email: stagons@hillsboroughcounty.org

Hope Center for Teens, Inc.
Joella Galvan
2650 Tinosa Circle
Pensacola, FL 32526

Sarasota Family YMCA
Jack Greer
One S School Avenue, Suite 301
Sarasota, FL 34237
Phone: (941) 951-2516

GEORGIA

Georgia Division of Family and Children
Services Independent Living Program
Walter C. Pitman, IL Coordinator
200 West Oglethorpe Boulevard
Albany, GA 31701
Phone: (229) 430-3385
Fax: (229) 430-4355
Email: wcpitman@dhr.state.ga.us

FYSB FUNDED TRANSITIONAL LIVING PROGRAMS (TLP)
Open Arms
Beth McKenzie
Rosalynn Fowler
Email: rosalynnfowler@hotmail.com
P.O. Box 71562
Albany, GA 31708
Phone: (229) 435-0979
Fax: (229) 435-5474

HAWAII

STATE COORDINATOR(S)
**Hawaii Department of Human Services,
Social Services Division**
Lee Dean, IL Coordinator
810 Richards Street, Suite 400
Honolulu, HI 96813
Phone: (808) 586-5704
Fax: (808) 586-4806
Email: ldean@dhs.state.hi.us

FYSB FUNDED TRANSITIONAL LIVING PROGRAMS (TLP)
Hale Kipa, Inc.
Jaque Kelly-Uyeoka
Email: jaq@halekipa.org
415 Keonianna St.
Honolulu, HI 96815
Phone: (808) 589-1829

Hawaii Youth Services Network
Judith Clark
677 Ala Moana Blvd., Suite 911
Honolulu, HI 96813
Phone: (808) 531-2198
Fax: (808) 524-3299
Email: hinet@pixi.com

IDAHO

STATE COORDINATOR(S)
Idaho Department of Health and Welfare
Lori Yellen, ILCoordinator
450 West State Street, 5th Floor
Boise, ID 83720
Phone: (208) 334-5695
Fax: (208) 334-6664
Email: YellenL@idhw.state.id.us

ILLINOIS

STATE COORDINATOR(S)
DCFS, Service Intervention
Kim Peck
Transitional Services Administrator
406 East Monroe Street, Station #22
Springfield, IL 62701
Phone: (217) 557-2689
Fax: (217) 557-5796
Email: kim.peck@illinois.gov

FYSB FUNDED TRANSITIONAL LIVING PROGRAMS (TLP)
Aunt Martha's
Gerald Garvey
233 West Joe Orr Road
Chicago Heights, IL 60411
Phone: (708) 754-1044
Email: amysc@enteract.com
Website: www.auntmarthas.org

Call for Help, Inc.
JoAnn Pisel, Executive Director
Pandora Harris, TLP Contact
9400 Lebanon Road
Edgemont, IL 62203
Phone: (618) 397-3076

Hoyleton Youth and Family Services
Chris Cox
8787 State Street
E. St. Louis, IL 62203
Phone: (618) 398-0900
Email: chris.cox@hoyleton.org

LePenseur Youth and Family Services
Reginald Summerrise
8550 South Manistee
Chicago , IL 60617

Project OZ
Peter Rankaitis
502 South Morris Avenue
Bloomington, IL 61701
Phone: (309) 827-0377

Rockford Meld, Inc.
Dawn Stanley
428 North First Street
Rockford, IL 61107
Phone: (815) 965-8336
Fax: (815) 965-9207
Email: meld@rockfordmeld.org
Website: www.rockfordmeld.org

**Teen Living Programs
(Foundation House)**
David Myers, Executive Director
3179 N. Broadway
Chicago, IL 60657
Phone: (773) 883-0085, ext. 18
Email: dmyers@teenliving.org

Youth Services of Illinois Valley
Dave McClure, Executive Director
Reggi Riley , TLP Contact
Email: rriley@ysbiv.org
424 West Madison Street
Ottawa, IL 61350
Phone: (815) 433-3953

INDIANA

STATE COORDINATOR(S)
Indiana Department of Child Services
Mary Lou Easter, IL Coordinator
20 West 2nd Street
Williamsport, IN 47993
Phone: (765) 762-6125
Fax: (765) 762-8017
Email: mary.easter@dcs.in.gov
Website: www.in.gov/dcs

FYSB FUNDED TRANSITIONAL LIVING PROGRAMS (TLP)
The Childrens Campus, Inc.
Patricia McLemore, Executive Director
Dr. Erin Curessy, TLP Contact
11411 Lincoln Way West
Mishawaka, IN 46544
Phone: (574) 259-5666
Email: infotcc@childrenscampus.org
Website: www.childrenscampus.org

IOWA

STATE COORDINATOR(S)
Iowa Department of Human Services
Holli Noble
Transition Planning Program Manager
Hoover State Office Building
Des Moines, IA 50319-0114
Phone: (515) 281-6786
Fax: (515) 281-4597
Email: hnoble@dhs.state.ia.us

FYSB FUNDED TRANSITIONAL LIVING PROGRAMS (TLP)
Foundation II
Steve Hartford
1630 1st Avenue NE, Suite 3
Cedar Rapids, IA 52405
Phone: (319) 368-3376
Fax: (319) 866-9603
Email: f2tlp@aol.com
Website: www.f2online.org
United Action for Youth
Jim Swaim
410 Iowa Avenue
Iowa City, IA 52244
Phone: (319) 338-7518

Youth and Shelter Services
George Belitsos
420 Kellogg
Ames, IA 50010
Phone: (515) 233-3141
Email: gbelitsos@yss.ames.ia.us
Website: www.yss.ames.ia.us

KENTUCKY

STATE COORDINATOR(S)
Kentucky Department for Community Based Services/Division of Protection and Permanency
Fawn Conley, IL Coordinator
275 East Main Street, Mail Stop 3C-E
Frankfort, KY 40621
Phone: (502) 564-2147
Fax: (502) 564-9554
Email: fawn.conley@mail.state.ky.us

FYSB FUNDED TRANSITIONAL LIVING PROGRAMS (TLP)
Presbyterian Child Welfare Agency
Buckhorn Children's Center
Bill McCarty
116 Buckhorn Lane
Buckhorn, KY 41721
Phone: (606) 398-7245
Email: bill.mccarty@buckhorn.org
Website: www.buckhorn.org

Volunteers of America, Kentucky
Joe Stevenson, Executive Director
Rebekah Lewis, TLP Contact
Email: rebekahl@voaky.org
P.O. Box 4011
Frankfurt, KY 40601
Phone: (505) 223-9821
Fax: (502) 223-9820

LOUISIANA

STATE COORDINATOR(S)
Louisiana Office of Community Services/Division of Social Services
Joe Bruno, Foster Care Manager
627 N 4th Street
Baton Rouge, LA 70802
Phone: (225) 342-4006
Fax: (225) 342-9087
Email: jbruno@dss.state.la.us

Louisiana Office of Community Services/Division of Social Services
Celeste Skinner, IL Coordinator
627 N 4th Street
Baton Rouge, LA 70802
Phone: (225) 342-4447
Fax: (225) 342-9087
Email: cskinner@dss.state.la.us

FYSB FUNDED TRANSITIONAL LIVING PROGRAMS (TLP)
Baton Rouge Alliance for Transitional Living
Bill Kwehn, Executive Director
260 South Acadian Trwy
Baton Rouge, LA 70806
Phone: (225) 343-6300
Email: billk@bratl.org

Education Treatment Council
Amy L. Dunn, Executive Director
P.O. Box 864
Lake Charles, LA 70602
Phone: (337) 433-1062
Fax: (337) 439-1094
Email: amy@etc-youth.org

Gulf Coast Teaching Family Service
Stacy Cradeur, Regional Director
154 North Hollywood Road
Houma, LA 70364
Email: scradeur@netzero.com

Our House, Inc.
Carol Christopher
P.O. Box 7496
Monroe, LA 71211
Phone: (318) 387-2186

MAINE

Bureau of Children & Family,
Maine Department of Human Services
Hugh E. Sipowicz, ILCoordinator
221 State Street, SHS #11
Augusta, ME 04333
Phone: (207) 287-6259
Fax: (207) 287-5282
Email: hugh.e.sipowicz@maine.gov

FYSB FUNDED TRANSITIONAL LIVING PROGRAMS (TLP)
Community Health & Counseling Services
Joseph Pickering, Executive Director
Dale Hamilton, TLP Contact
P.O. Box 425
Bangor, ME 04402-0425
Phone: (207) 947-0366
Email: summer@chcs-me.org

Good Will Home Association
Michael Hinckley-Gordon,
Director of TLP Programs
P.O. Box 159
Hinckley, ME 04944-0159
Phone: (207) 238-4000
Email: MHinckley-Gordon@gwh.org

New Beginnings
Bob Rowe, Executive Director
Email: bobrowe@gwi.net
Mary Ruchinskas, Development Director
Email: maryru@gwi.net
436 Main Street
Lewiston, ME 04240
Phone: (207) 795-4077

Stepping Stones
Luetta Goodall
P.O. Box 189
Houlton, ME 04730
Phone: (207) 532-9358
Email: luettag@stepstones4youth.org
Website: www.stepstones4youth.org

MARYLAND

STATE COORDINATOR(S)
Maryland Department of Human Services
Dianne Timmons-Himes
State IL Coordinator
311 West Saratoga Street, 5th flr, Room 547
Baltimore, MD 21201
Phone: (410) 767-7114
Fax: (410) 333-0127
Email: dthimes@dhr.state.md.us

FYSB FUNDED TRANSITIONAL LIVING PROGRAMS (TLP)
Hearts and Homes for Youth, Inc.
Michael Stern, Michelle Sewell
1320 Fenwick Lane, Suite 800
Silver Spring, MD 20910
Phone: (301) 589-8444
Email: msewell@hh4y.org

MASSACHUSETTS

STATE COORDINATOR(S)
Massachusetts Department of Social Services
Maureen Fallon Messeder
Associate Director Adolescent Services
24 Farnsworth Street
Boston, MA 02210
Phone: (617) 748-2231
Fax: (617) 748-2311
Email: maureen.messeder@state.ma.us

FYSB FUNDED TRANSITIONAL LIVING PROGRAMS (TLP)
Bridge Over Troubled Waters, Inc
Sheila Moore, Executive Director
Marylyn Rogers, Program Director
47 West Street
Boston, MA 02111
Phone: (617) 423-9575
Email: bridgeotw@gis.net
Website: www.bridgeovertroubledwater.org

Catholic Charitable Bureau of the Archdiocese of Boston
Joseph Doolin
75 Kneeland Street, 8th flr.
Boston, MA 02111
Phone: (617) 482-5440

L.U.K. Crisis Center
Lois Barry, CEO
99 Day Street
Fitchburg, MA 01420
Phone: (978) 345-0685
Email: lbarry@luk.org
Website: www.luk.org

Life Resources, Inc. Promising Futures
Dawn Haynes, TLP Contact
686 North Main Street
Brockton, MA 02301
Phone: (508) 584-3855
Email: promisingfuturespd@liferesourcesinc.org

ServiceNet, Inc.
Susan Stubbs, CEO
129 King Street
Northampton, MA 01060
Phone: (413) 586-8680
Website: www.servicenetinc.org

Wayside Youth and Family Support Network, Inc
Eric LeMasi
75 Fountain Street
Framingham, MA 01701
Phone: (508) 879-8900 ext. 222

MICHIGAN

STATE COORDINATOR(S)
Michigan Department of Social Services
Shannon Gibson, IL Coordinator
235 South Grand, Suite 510
Lansing, MI 48909
Phone: (517) 241-8904
Fax: (517) 335-7047
Email: gibsons3@michigan.gov

FYSB FUNDED TRANSITIONAL LIVING PROGRAMS (TLP)
Alternatives for Girls
Patty Swift, TLP Contact
903 West Grand Blvd. 1
Detroit, MI 48208
Phone: (313) 361-4000
Fax: (313) 361-8938
Email: pswift@alternativesforgirls.org
Website: www.alternativesforgirls.org

Catholic Family Services
Frances Denny
1819 Gull Road
Kalamazoo, MI 49048
Phone: (269) 381-9800
Email: frandenny@catholicfamilyservices.org

Common Ground Sanctuary
James A. Perlaki
1410 South Telegraph
Bloomfield Hill, MI 48302
Phone: (248) 456-8150
Fax: (248) 456-8147
Email: jperlaki@commongroundsanctuary.org
Website: www.commongroundsanctuary.org

Comprehensive Youth Services
(Macomb Co. Youth Interim Care Facility)
Joanne Smyth
2 Crocker Blvd., Suite 103
Mt. Clemens, MI 48043-2558
Phone: (586) 463-7079

Every Woman's Place
Mary MacDonald, Executive Director
Lori Trautner, TLP Contact
1221 West Laketon
Muskegon, MI 49441
Phone: (616) 726-4493 ext. 255
Phone: (231) 759-7909
Email: ewpmuskego@aol.com

Listening Ear Crisis Center d.b.a.
Al Kaufman Jr., Director
107 East Illiniois
Mt. Pleasant, MI 48858
Phone: (989) 773-6904 ext. 235
Email: kaufmann@listeningear.com
Website: www.listeningear.com

Lutheran Social Services Of Wisconsin and Upper Michigan
Beth Davis
Email: bdavis@lsswis.org
Website: www.lsswis.org

Ozone House
Mary Jo Campbell, Executive Director
1705 Washtenaw Avenue
Ann Arbor, MI 48104
Phone: (734) 662-2265
Email: kdoyle@ozonehouse.org
Website: www.ozonehouse.org

Ruth Ellis Center
Grace A. McCelland, Executive Director
2727 Second Ave., Suite 158
Detroit, MI 48201
Phone: (313) 964-2091
Fax: (313) 964-3372
Email: grace.mccelland@ruthelliscenter.com
Website: www.ruthelliscenter.com

Saginaw County Youth Council
Ronald Spess
P.O. Box 3191
Saginaw, MI 48605
Phone: (517) 752-5175
Email: innerlink@chartermi.net

Traverse Place Genesee County Youth Corporation
Cassandra Wolford
512 South Grand Traverse
Flint, MI 48502
Phone: (810) 341-6328
Fax: (810) 341-6757
Email: tlp@intouchmi.com

MINNESOTA

STATE COORDINATOR(S)
Minnesota Department of Human Services, Family and Children's Services
Claire Hill, ILCoordinator
444 Lafayette Road
St. Paul, MN 55155-3832
Phone: (651) 296-4471
Fax: (651) 297-1949
Email: claire.d.hill@state.mn.us

FYSB FUNDED TRANSITIONAL LIVING PROGRAMS (TLP)
Ain Dah Yung Shelter (Our Home Center)
Gabrielle Strong
1089 Portland Avenue
St. Paul, MN 55104
Phone: (651) 227-4184

Catholic Charities of St. Paul
Cheryl Carrigan
1121 East 46th Street
Minneapolis, MN 55407
Phone: (612) 827-6241

Dakota County
Jane Lawrenz
1 Mendota Road West, #500
West St. Paul, MN 55118
Phone: (651) 554-5759
Fax: (651) 554-5808
Email: jane.lawrenz@co.dakota.mn.us

Lutheran Social Services of Minnesota
Ellen Erickson
1299 Arcade
St. Paul, MN 55106

Lutheran Social Services of Minnesota
Jane Hopkins
803 Kingwood, 4th Floor
Brainerd, MN 56401
Phone: (218) 828-4399

The Bridge
Ed Murphy, Executive Director
Beth Holger
2200 Emerson Avenue S.
Minneapolis, MN 55405
Phone: (612) 377-8800
Fax: (612) 377-6426
Email: bholger@bridgeforyouth.org
Website: www.bridgeforyouth.org

MISSISSIPPI

STATE COORDINATOR(S)
Mississippi Department of Human Resources
Sergio A. Trejo, IL Coordinator
750 North State Street
Jackson, MS 39205
Phone: (601) 359-4983
Fax: (601) 359-2525
Email: strejo@mdhs.state.ms.us

FYSB FUNDED TRANSITIONAL LIVING PROGRAMS (TLP)
Southern Christian Services for Children and Youth, Inc.
Sue Cherney
1900 N. West Street, Suite B
Jackson, MS 39202-1033
Phone: (601) 354-0983
Email: scssue@aol.com

MONTANA

STATE COORDINATOR(S)
Montana Department of Human Services
Heather Winters, IL Coordinator
1400 Broadway, RM C118, Cogswell Bldg
Helena, MT 59604-8005
Phone: (406) 444-4191
Fax: (406) 444-5956
Email: hwinters@mt.gov

FYSB FUNDED TRANSITIONAL LIVING PROGRAMS (TLP)
Montana Human Resources Development Council Directors
Maggie Driscoll
1801 South Higgins
Missoula, MT 59801
Phone: (406) 728-3710
Fax: (406) 728-7680
Email: mag@hccxi.org

Tumbleweed Runaway Program
Sally Habeck
3311 4th Avenue North, Suite 5
Billings, MT 59101-1268
Phone: (406) 259-2558

NEBRASKA

STATE COORDINATOR(S)
Health and Human Services
Mark Mitchell, IL Coordinator
301 Centennial Mall South
Lincoln, NE 68509
Phone: (402) 471-9211
Fax: (402) 471-9034
Email: mark.mitchell@hhss.ne.us

FYSB FUNDED TRANSITIONAL LIVING PROGRAMS (TLP)
Cedars Youth Services
James Blue,
620 N. 48th Street, Suite 100
Lincoln, NE 68504
Phone: (402) 466-6181
Email: info@cedars-kids.org

Omaha Home for Boys
Willie Bob Johnson
Email: williebobj@omahahomeforboys.org
4343 North 52nd Street
Omaha, NE 68104
Phone: (402) 457-7195

Panhandle Community Services
Jan Fitts
3350 North 10th Street
Gering, NE 69341
Phone: (308) 635-3089

NEVADA

STATE COORDINATOR(S)
Division of Children & Family Services
Hayley Jarolimek, IL Coordinator
4220 South Maryland Parkway,
Bldg B, Suite 300
Las Vegas, NV 89119
Phone: (702) 486-7668
Fax: (702) 486-7626
Email: hjarolim@dcfs.state.nv.us

NEW HAMPSHIRE

STATE COORDINATOR(S)
NH Division of Children, Youth and Families
Rob Rodler, IL Program Specialist
Brown Building, 4th Floor
129 Pleasant Street
Concord, NH 03301-3857
Phone: (603) 271-4706
Fax: (603) 271-4729
Email: rrodler@dhhs.state.nh.us

FYSB FUNDED TRANSITIONAL LIVING PROGRAMS (TLP)
Child and Family Services
Michael Ostrowski, President
Email: ostrowskim@cfsnh.org
Gale Starr, TLP Contact
Email: starrg@cfsnh.org
99 Hanover Street
Manchester, NH 03105
Phone: (603) 668-1920
Website: www.cfsnh.org

NEW MEXICO

STATE COORDINATOR(S)
Protective Services
Ceslie Griggs, Program Manager
1120 Paseo De Peralta
Pera Building, Room 254
Santa Fe, NM 87502
Phone: (505) 476-1046
Fax: (505) 827-8433
Email: cgriggs@cyfd.state.nm.us

FYSB FUNDED TRANSITIONAL LIVING PROGRAMS (TLP)
Families and Youth, Inc.
Bernadette Torres
Email: btorres@fyinm.org
Dana Malone, TLP Contact
Email: Dmalone@fyinm.org
880 East Idaho
Las Cruces, NM 88001
Phone: (505) 523-0572
Fax: (505) 527-4457
Website: www.fyinm.org

The Dream Tree Project
Kim Treiber
P.O. Box 1677, 128 La Posta Road
Taos, NM 87571
Phone: (505) 758-9595
Email: dtp@laplaza.org
Website: www.dreamtreeproject.org

Youth Shelters and Family Services—Casa Libertad TLP
Tiffany Lewis, TLP Contact
224 N. Guadalupe Street
Santa Fe, NM 87507
Phone: (505) 955-1684
Email: tlewis@youthshelters.org

NEW YORK

STATE COORDINATOR(S)

Office of Strategic Planning & Policy Development New York State Office of Children & Family Services
Nancy White Martinez, Director
Capital View Office Park, Room 313
South 52 Washington Street
Rensselaer, NY 12144
Phone: (518) 473-1776
Fax: (518) 473-2410
Email: Nancy.Martinez@ocfs.state.ny.us

FYSB FUNDED TRANSITIONAL LIVING PROGRAMS (TLP)

Chautauqua Opportunities
Bill Vogt, TLP Contact
Email: bvogt@chautopp.org
16 East Sixth Street
Jamestown , NY 14701
Phone: (716) 661-9446
Fax: (716) 661-9448
Email: safehouse@madbbs.com
Website:
www.chautauquaopportunities.com

Equinox, Inc.
Mary Campagna
95 Central Avenue
Albany, NY 12206
Phone: (518) 434-6135
Fax: (518) 434-4502
Email: mcampagna@equinoxinc.org
Website: www.equinoxinc.org

Family and Children's Association
Richard Bell
Christina Alonso, TLP Contact
100 East Old Country Road
Mineola, NY 11501
Phone: (516) 485-4600
Fax: (516) 221-1844

Family of Woodstock
Michael Berg
P.O. Box 3516, 39 John Street
Kingston, NY 12402
Phone: (914) 331-7080

Green Chimneys Children's Services
Theresa Nolan
456 West 145th Street, Suite 1
New York, NY 10031
Phone: (212) 491-5911 ext. 19
Fax: (212) 368-8975
Website: www.greenchimneys.org

Hillside Children's Center
Tess Mahnken-Weatherspoon
1183 Monroe Avenue
Rochester, NY 14620-1699
Phone: (585) 256-7500
Fax: (585) 654-4506
Email: tmahnken@hillside.com

Hudson River Housing, Inc.
Corinne Lesko, TLP Contact
Email: clesko@hudsonriverhousing.org
Patrice Kellett,
Email: pkellett@hudsonriverhousing.org
305-307 Mill Street
Poughkeepsie, NY 12601
Phone: (845) 454-2300
Fax: (845) 485-1641
Website: www.hudsonriverhousing.org

Mohawk Valley Community Action Agency
Kelly Fleming, TLP Contact
207 North James Street
Rome, NY 13440
Phone: (315) 339-4960
Fax: (315) 339-2981
Email: kfleming@mvcaa.com
Website: www.mvcaa.com

Oswego County Opportunities
Sarah Irland
75 East 1st Street, Midtown Plaza
Oswego, NY 13126
Phone: (315) 342-7532
Fax: (315) 342-7554
Email: sirland@oco.org
Website: www.oco.org

Services for Youth
Rose W. Washington
Michael Danenberg, TLP Contact
Email: mdanenberg@berkshirefarm.org
13640 Route 22
Canaan, NY 12029
Phone: (518) 781-4567
Website: www.berkshirefarm.org

The Center for Youth Services
Dr. Elaine Spaull, Executive Director
Pat Johnson, TLP Contact
Email: pjohnson@centerforyouth.net
258 Alexander Street
Rochester, NY 14607
Phone: (716) 473-2464

The Children's Village
Aron Myers
Echo Hills, Dobbs Ferry, NY 10522
Phone: (914) 593-0667
Email: amyers@childrensvillage.org
Website: www.childrensvillage.org
The Salvation Army
Tom Roshau
Email: troshau315@aol.com
677 S. Salina Street
Syracuse, NY 13202
Phone: (315) 479-1353

Westhab, Inc.
Robert Miller
85 Executive Boulevard
Elmsford, NY 10523
Phone: (914) 345-2800
Email: bobmiller@westhab.org
Website: www.westhab.org

NORTH CAROLINA

STATE COORDINATOR(S)
North Carolina Division of Social Services
Joan S. McAllister
State Coordinator NC LINKS
MSC 2409
325 North Salisbury Street
Raleigh, NC 27699-2409
Phone: (919) 733-2580
Fax: (919) 715-0766
Email: joan.mcallister@ncmail.net
Website:
www.dhhs.state.nc.us/dss/c_srv/cserv_ind.htm
at 1-800-820-0001. www.saysoinc.org

FYSB FUNDED TRANSITIONAL LIVING PROGRAMS (TLP)
CARING for Children, Inc. (Trinity Place)
John Lauterbach
P.O. Box 19113
Asheville, NC 28815
Phone: (828) 298-0186
Email: caring4children@charter.net

Haven House
Matt Schnars
706 Hillsborough Street, Suite 102
Raleigh, NC 27603
Phone: (919) 833-3312
Email: mschnars@havenhousenc.org
Website: www.havenhousenc.org

With Friends, Inc.
Patricia A. Krikorian
P.O. Box 971
Belmont, NC 28012
Phone: (704) 866-7774
Email: patkrikorian@aol.com
Website: www.withfriendsyouthshelter.org

Youth Focus, Inc
Charles Hodierne
715 N. Eugene Street
Greensboro, NC 27401
Phone: (336) 274-5909
Email: chodierne@youthfocus.org
Website: www.youthfocus.org

OHIO

STATE COORDINATOR(S)

Child Protection and Placement Services
Carrie Anthony, Section Chief
P.O. Box 182709
Columbus, OH 43218-2709
Phone: (614) 752-6208
Fax: (614) 466-0164
Email: Anthoc@odjfs.state.oh.us

FYSB FUNDED TRANSITIONAL LIVING PROGRAMS (TLP)

Bellefaire JCB
Adam G. Jacobs, Executive Director
Email: senters@bellefairejcb.org
Bob Schuppel,, TLP Contact
Email: senters@bellefairejcb.org
22001 Fairmount Boulevard
Cleveland, OH 44118
Phone: (216) 932-2800
Phone: (216) 320-8484
Website: bellefairejcb.org

Daybreak, Inc.
Linda L. Cramer, Executive Director
50 Theobald Court
Dayton, OH 45410
Phone: (937) 461-1000
Email: wilsonl@daybreakdayton.org
Email: sewardl@daybreakdayton.org

Huckleberry House
Carrie Mularz
1421 Hamlet Street
Columbus, OH 43201
Phone: (614) 294-8097
Fax: (614) 294-6109
Email: cmularz@huckhouse.org
Website: www.huckhouse.org

Lighthouse Youth Services
Mark Kroner
Director of Self-Sufficiency Division
1501 Madison Road
Cincinnati, OH 45206
Phone: (513) 487-7130
Fax: (513) 475-5689
Email: mkroner@lyl.org
Website: www.lys.org

P.A.L. Mission
Jill Miller, Executive Director
1634 Market Avenue South
Canton, OH 44707
Phone: (330) 453-9199
Fax: (330) 453-9219
Email: pal4599@sssnet.com
Website: www.palmission.org

Sojourners Care Network
Ephraim Kotey, TLP Contact
P.O. Box 312
McArthur, OH 45701
Phone: (740) 596-2164
Email: newroads@sojournerscare.net
Website: www.sojournerscare.net

OKLAHOMA

STATE COORDINATOR(S)
Oklahoma Department of Human Services
Cathy Connelly, IL Coordinator
2400 North Lincoln Boulevard
Sequoyah Building
Oklahoma City, OK 73105
Phone: (405) 521-6671
Fax: (405) 521-4373
Email: cathy.connelly@okdhs.org
Website: http://www.okdhs.org/
programsandservices/il/

Oklahoma Department of Human Services
Clay Zahn, IL Coordinator
2400 North Lincoln Boulevard
Sequoyah Building
Oklahoma City, OK 73105
Phone: (405) 521-4077
Fax: (405) 521-4373
Email: clay.zahn@okdhs.org
Website: http://www.okdhs.org/programsand
services/il/

FYSB FUNDED TRANSITIONAL LIVING PROGRAMS (TLP)
Cherokee Nation Youth Services
Linda Vann, Executive Director
Email: Linda-Vann@cherokee.org
Fran Simms, TLP Contact
Email: Fran-Simms@cherokee.org
P.O. Box 948
Tahlequah, OK 74465
Phone: (918) 456-0671 ext. 2787

Payne County Youth Services
Shirley Mitchell,
Director of TLP Programs
Email: pcystlp@msn.com
Tim Whaley, Executive Director
Email: tim@pcys.org
2224 West 12th, P.O. Box 2647
Stillwater, OK 74076
Phone: (405) 377-3380
Website: www.pcys.org

Southwestern Youth Services
Judie M. Hanes, Executive Director
P.O. Box 175, 1313 North Forrest
Altus, OK 73522-0175
Phone: (580) 482-6229
Email: swys@sbcglobal.net

The Chickasaw Nation
Jay Keel
Email: Regina.Pereira2@chickasaw.net
Chris Redman, TLP Contact
Email: chris.redman@chickasaw.net
P.O. Box 1548
Ada, OK 74821-1548
Phone: (580) 226-4869

Youth and Family Services
Dee Blose, Executive Director
2404 Sunset Drive
El Reno, OK 73036
Phone: (405) 262-6555

Youth Services of Tulsa
James M. Walker, Executive Director
Email: jwalker@yst.org
Amy Redus, TLP Contact
Email: aredus@yst.org
311 South Madison
Tulsa, OK 74120
Phone: (918) 582-0061
Website: www.yst.org

OREGON

DHS—Independent Living Program, E76
Rosemary Iavenditti
ILP Fiscal Coordinator
500 Summer Street NE
Salem, OR 97301-1069
Phone: (503) 945-5688
Fax: (503) 945-6969
Email: rosemary.iavenditti@state.or.us
Website: www.dhs.state.or.us/children/
fostercare/ind_living/ilp.htm

FYSB FUNDED TRANSITIONAL LIVING PROGRAMS (TLP)

J Bar J Ranch
Stephanie Alvstad
62895 Hamby Road
Bend, OR 97701
Phone: (541) 389-1409
Email: Stephanie Alvstad

Janus Youth Programs
Dennis Morrow, Executive Director
707 NE Couch Street
Portland, OR 97232
Phone: (503) 233-6090
Fax: (503) 233-6093

Looking Glass Youth and Family Services-New Roads Program
Craig Opperman, Executive Director
Eric VanHouten, TLP Contact
Email: eric.vanhouten@lookingglass.us
72-B Centennial Loop, Suite 2
Eugene, OR 97401
Phone: (541) 686-2688
Fax: (541) 345-7605
Website: www.lookingglass.us

Northwest Human Services
Paul Logan, Executive Director
681 Center Street NE
Salem, OR 97301
Phone: (503) 588-5828
Email: jplumb@nwhumanservices.org

Outside In
Kathy J. Oliver
1132 SW 13th Avenue
Portland, OR 97205
Phone: (503) 223-4121
Email: koliver@outsidein.org

The Boys and Girls Aid Society of Oregon
Donna McClung, TLP Contact
018 S.W. Boundary Court
Portland, OR 97239
Phone: (503) 542-2365
Email: dmcclung@boysandgirlsaid.org
Website: www.boysandgirlsaid.org

PENNSYLVANIA

STATE COORDINATOR(S)
Department of Public Welfare/
Office of Children, Youth and Families
Angelo Santore, IL Coordinator
1401 North 7th Street
Bertolino Building, 4th Floor
Harrisburg, PA 17105-2675
Phone: (717) 772-7012
Fax: (717) 214-3784
Email: asantore@state.pa.us

FYSB FUNDED TRANSITIONAL LIVING PROGRAMS (TLP)
Centre County Youth Service
Norma Keller
410 South Fraser Street
State College, PA 16801
Phone: (814) 237-5731
Email: ysb@ccysb.com
Website: www.ccysb.com

CH Pennsylvania Under 21
Jerome Kilbane
417 Callowhill Street
Philadelphia, PA 19123

Northern Cambria Community
Development Corporation
Connie Kuzma
4200 Crawford Avenue, Suite 200
Northern Cambria, PA 15714
Phone: (814) 948-4444
Email: ncamcfr@shopsurf.net

Three Rivers Youth
Peggy B. Harris
2039 Termon Avenue
Pittsburgh, PA 15212
Phone: (412) 766-2215
Email: tryyouth@aol.com

RHODE ISLAND

STATE COORDINATOR(S)
Rhode Island DCFS
John P. O'Riley, IL Coordinator
101 Friendship Street
Providence, RI 02903
Phone: (401) 528-3764
Fax: (401) 528-3780
Email: john.o'riley@dcyf.ri.gov

FYSB FUNDED TRANSITIONAL LIVING PROGRAMS (TLP)
The Urban League of Rhode Island
Sara Dionne, TLP Contact
246 Prairie Avenue
Providence, RI 02905
Phone: (401) 351-5000 ext. 112
Email: sara@ulri.org

SOUTH CAROLINA

STATE COORDINATOR(S)
South Carolina Department of Social
Services
Helen Pridgen, IL Coordinator
P.O. Box 1520
1535 Confederate Avenue
Columbia, SC 29202-1520
Phone: (803) 898-7571
Fax: (803) 898-7641
Email: hpridgen@dss.state.sc.us

FYSB FUNDED TRANSITIONAL LIVING PROGRAMS (TLP)
Sea Haven, Inc.
Christina Jackson
P.O. Box 600
N. Myrtle Beach, SC 29597
Phone: (843) 399-4045
Email: cbjack@sccoast.net
Website: www.seahaveninc.com

TENNESSEE

STATE COORDINATOR(S)

Tennessee Department of Children's Services
Lane Simpson, IL Director
Menzler 1, 1280 Foster Avenue
Nashville, TN 34243
Phone: (615) 253-0024
Fax: (615) 253-2272
Email: lane.simpson@state.tn.us
Website: www.state.tn.us/youth/

FYSB FUNDED TRANSITIONAL LIVING PROGRAMS (TLP)

Oasis Center, Inc.
Hal Cato, Executive Director
Michelle Hall, TLP Contact
Email: MHall@oasiscenter.org
1221 16th Avenue South
Nashville, TN 37212
Phone: (615) 327-4455
Email: oasis@oasiscenter.org
Website: www.oasiscenter.org

TEXAS

STATE COORDINATOR(S)

Lead Program Specialist, Transitioning Youth Services
Candice Holmes
Transitioning Youth Specialist Lead
701 West 51st Street, MC W-157
Austin, TX 78751
Phone: (512) 438-2350
Fax: (512) 438-3782
Email: candice.holmes@dfps.state.tx.us
Website:
www.tdprs.state.tx.us/Child_Protection/
Preparation_For_Adult_Living/

Texas Department of Family and Protective Services
Gaye Vopat, PAL Program Specialist
701 West 51st Street, MC W-157
Austin, TX 78751
Phone: (512) 438-5442
Fax: (512) 438-3782
Email: gaye.vopat@dfps.state.tx.us
Website:
www.tdprs.state.tx.us/Child_Protection/
Preparation_For_Adult_Living/

Texas Department of Family and Protective Services
David Smith, ETV Program Specialist
701 West 51st Street, MC W-157
Austin, TX 78751
Phone: (512) 438-3144
Fax: (512) 438-3782
Email: david.smith@dfps.state.tx.us

FYSB FUNDED TRANSITIONAL LIVING PROGRAMS (TLP)

Central Texas Youth Services Bureau
Steve Wick, Deputy Director
204 North East Street
Bolton, TX 76513
Phone: (254) 939-3466
Email: ctysbtx@swbell.net
Website:
www.centraltexasyouthservices.org

Collin Intervention to Youth
Linda Goodman, TLP Contact
Email: lgoodmancityhouse@earthlink.net
3200 Stonecrest
Plano, TX 75074
Phone: (972) 423-7057
Fax: (972) 578-6660
Email: tccpres@aol.com
Website: www.cityhouse.org

Connections Individual and Family Services, Inc.
Kellie Stalllings
1414 W San Antonio Street
New Braunfels, TX 78130
Phone: (830) 629-6571
Email: kstallings_cifs@ev1.net
Website: www.connectionsnonprofit.org

Crossroads Youth and Family Services
Stan Hamlyn
P.O. Box 436
Victoria, TX 77902

DePelchin Children's Center
Jane Harding
100 Sandman
Houston, TX 77007
Phone: (713) 802-7733
Email: jharding@depelchin.org

El Paso Center for Children
Jeanne Hosch, TLP Contact
2200 N. Stevens
El Paso, TX 79930
Phone: (915) 565-8361
Email: jhosch@whc.net

Faith Walk
Yolanda Mitchell
1148 S. Joe Wilson Road
Cedar Hill, TX 75104

George Gervin Youth Center
Barbara D. Hawkins
6903 Sunbelt Drive South
San Antonio, TX 78218
Phone: (210) 804-1786
Email: barbara.hawkins@gervin-school.org

Marywood
Jean Henry, TLP Contact
510 West 26th Street
Austin , TX 78705
Phone: (512) 472-9251
Fax: (512) 472-4829
Email: jhenry@marywood.org
Website: www.marywood.org

Promise House
Patty Parker
Regina Sylvester, Program Manager
236 West Page Street
Dallas, TX 75208-6631
Phone: (214) 941-8578
Email: contact@promisehouse.org
Website: www.promisehouse.org

Roy Maas' Youth Alternatives
Kat Golando, TLP Contact
3103 West Avenue
San Antonio, TX 78213
Phone: (210) 340-7933
Email: kgolando@rmya-sa.org

The Childrens Center, Inc.
James T. Kell
P.O. Box 2600
Galveston, TX 77553-2600
Phone: (409) 765-5212
Fax: (409) 765-6094
Website: www.thechildrenscenterinc.org

Youth and Family Alliance
Mitch Weynand, Director,
Administrative Services COO
Email: mitch.weynand@lifeworksweb.org
Steve Bewsey, TLP Contact
Email: steve.bewsey@lifeworksweb.org
1221 W. Ben White Boulevard,
Suite 108A
Austin , TX 78704
Phone: (512) 735-2200
Website: www.lifeworksweb.org

UTAH

STATE COORDINATOR(S)
**Utah Department of Human Services,
Division of Children and Family Services**
Pamela Russell, IL Coordinator
120 North 200 West, Room 225
Salt Lake City, UT 84103
Phone: (801) 538-4308
Fax: (801) 538-3993
Email: pkrussel@utah.gov

FYSB FUNDED TRANSITIONAL LIVING PROGRAMS (TLP)
Volunteers of America, Utah
Jeff St. Romain, Executive Director
Nicole Campolucci, TLP Contact
Email: ncampolucci@voaut.org
718 South 600 East
Salt Lake City, UT 84102
Phone: (801) 359-5545
Fax: (801) 363-9414
Website: www.voaut.org

VERMONT

STATE COORDINATOR(S)

Vermont Department of Social Services
Dana Lawrence
Director of Program Management
103 South Main
Osgood Building
Waterbury, VT 05676
Phone: (802) 241-2407
Fax: (802) 241-2980
Email: dana.lawrence@ahs.state.vt.us

Department for Children & Families
Family Services Division
Katherine Boise
State Youth Development Coordinator
Osgood Office Complex Building, 3rd floor
103 South Main Street
Waterbury, VT 05671-2401
Phone: (802) 241-1507
Fax: (802) 244-2407
Email: katherineboise@ahs.state.vt.us

Department for Children and Families,
Family Services Division
Jan Levins, Program Manager
Osgood Office Complex Building, 3rd floor
103 South Main Street
Waterbury, VT 05671-2401
Phone: (802) 241-2131
Fax: (802) 244-2407
Email: jan.levins@ahs.state.vt.us

FYSB FUNDED TRANSITIONAL LIVING PROGRAMS (TLP)

Spectrum Youth and Family Services
Mark Redmond,
31 Elmwood Avenue
Burlington, VT 05401
Phone: (802) 864-7423 ext. 209
Email: sjolles@spectrumvt.org

Vermont Coalition of Runaway and
Homeless Youth Programs, Washington
County Youth Services Bureau
Kreig Pinkhem, TLP Contact
P.O. Box 627, 38 Elm Street
Montpelier, VT 25601
Phone: (802) 229-9151
Email: kpinkem@adelphia.net

WASHINGTON

STATE COORDINATOR(S)

Washington Children's Administration
Rick Butt, IL Program Manager
1115 Washington Street
P.O. Box 45710
Olympia, WA 98504-5710
Phone: (206) 923-4891
Fax: (360) 902-7903
Email: rlbu300@dshs.wa.gov
Website: www1.dshs.wa.gov/

FYSB FUNDED TRANSITIONAL LIVING PROGRAMS (TLP)

Community Youth Services
Charles Shelan, Executive Director
711 State Avenue NE
Olympia, WA 98506
Phone: (360) 943-0780
Email: info@communityyouthservices.org
Website: www.communityyouth
services.org

Friends of Youth
Ed Belleba, Executive Director
Kelly Land , TLP Contact
Email: kelly@friendsofyouth.org
16225 NE 87th Street, Suite A-6
Redmond, WA 98052
Phone: (425) 869-6490 ext. 320
Fax: (425) 869-6666
Website: www.friendsofyouth.org

Northwest Youth Services
David Webster
1020 North State Street
Bellingham, WA 98225
Phone: (360) 734-9862
Email: kathyb-nwys@uswest.net

Volunteers of America Spokane
Marilee K. Roloff
Heidi Peterson, TLP Contact
Email: hpeterson@voaspokane.org
525 West Second Avenue
Spokane, WA 99201
Phone: (509) 624-2378

YouthCare
Bill Wilson
Email: bill.Wilson@youthcare.org
Katie Grossman, TLP Contact
Email: Katie.Grossman@YouthCare.org
2500 NE 54th Street, Suite 100
Seattle, WA 98105
Phone: (206) 604-4500 ext. 1213

WISCONSIN

STATE COORDINATOR(S)
Wisconsin Department of Health and Family Services
Christine Lenske, IL Coordinator
P.O. Box 8916
One West Wilson, Room 527
Madison, WI 53708
Phone: (608) 267-7287
Fax: (608) 264-6750
Email: lenskca@dhfs.state.wi.us
Website:
www.dhfs.state.wi.us/Children/IndLiving/index.HTM

Department of Health and Family Services
June Paul, IL and Kinship Coordinator
P.O. Box 8916
One West Wilson, Room 527
Madison, WI 53708-8916
Phone: (608) 267-7287
Fax: (608) 264-6750
Email: paulj@dhfs.state.wi.us
Website:
www.dhfs.state.wi.us/Children/IndLiving/index.HTM

FYSB FUNDED TRANSITIONAL LIVING PROGRAMS (TLP)
Christian Group Home, Inc.
Zonica Zindler
840 N. Taylor Street
Green Bay, WI 54303

Innovative Youth Services
James Huycke
1030 Washington Avenue
Racine, WI 53403
Phone: (414) 632-0424

Lutheran Social Services of Wisconsin and Upper Michigan
Marilyn Page
1337 Taylor Street, Suite 104
Sheboygan, WI 53081
Phone: (920) 458-8381

Northeast Wisconsin, Inc.
Thomas Martin
300 Crooks Street
Green Bay, WI 54313
Phone: (920) 436-6800
Email: tl@familservicesnew.org
Website: www.familyservicesnew.org

Up Connections, Inc.
Jenifer Finley
4334 Madison Street
Waukesha, WI 53188

Walker's Point Youth and Family Center
Andre Olton
2030 W. National Avenue
Milwaukee, WI 53204
Phone: (414) 672-5300

WYOMING

STATE COORDINATOR(S)
Wyoming Department of Family Services
Diana Schafer, IL Coordinator
130 Hobbs Avenue
Cheyenne, WY 82009
Phone: (307) 777-6348
Fax: (307) 777-3693
Email: dschaf@state.wy.us

Wyoming Division of Social Services
Zaffer Sharif, IL Coordinator
130 Hobbs Avenue
Cheyenne, WY 82009
Phone: (307) 777-6203
Fax: (307) 777-3693
Email: zshari@state.wy.us

Source: National Child Welfare Resource Center
For Youth Development www.nrcys.ou.edu/yd/

ABOUT THE AUTHOR

Charisse Nesbit is a writer and former foster child who received an M.F.A. degree in Creative Writing from Columbia College in Chicago. She hopes to inspire other foster children through her writing work and personal accomplishments. She currently resides in Los Angeles where she is working in the film industry. You may visit her at www.myspace.com/ajoyachieved or at www.ajoyachieved.com.